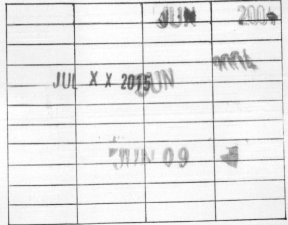
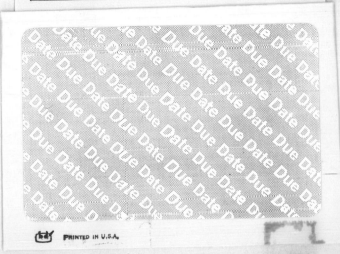

ESSAYS AND STUDIES
1964

Shakespeare Quatercentenary Edition

ESSAYS AND STUDIES
1964

BEING VOLUME SEVENTEEN OF THE NEW SERIES
OF ESSAYS AND STUDIES COLLECTED FOR
THE ENGLISH ASSOCIATION
BY WILLIAM A. ARMSTRONG

NEW YORK: HUMANITIES PRESS

Printed in Great Britain by
Cox & Wyman Ltd., London, Fakenham and Reading

Contents

▼

Plates

NOTE. References throughout are to *The Tudor Edition of William Shakespeare: The Complete Works*, edited by Peter Alexander, London 1951

I

Language in 'Love's Labour's Lost'

WILLIAM MATTHEWS

No less than the professional linguist, a writer is a student of the language he uses: indeed, it might be argued that his exemplary craft, particularly if he be a playwright and a poet-playwright, demands a subtler and more comprehensive study of language than does the analytical and anatomical craft of the linguist. The writer may have no adeptness in categorizing or describing the present or past of the phonology, morphology, syntax, and lexicon that constitute the tools of his trade, but the demands of extended exemplification ensure that he will be keenly aware of the varieties and details of individual usage, ready in exploiting them, even of extending them, and sensitive to linguistic shifts of all kinds, social and fashionable as well as historic. And since language is the tool by which the writer lives, he is likely to be seriously concerned with its values and validity and with what is happening to it. The scientific linguist may pride himself upon being an impartial observer of a linguistic system—one reason perhaps why he has tended towards the past or the alien in language; but the inclination of the writer is to be a linguistic critic and sometimes a reformer or guardian of the language he uses.

All Shakespeare's plays exhibit his resource in language, his delight in exploiting its resources, and his preoccupation with its strengths and weaknesses; but it is in *Love's Labour's Lost* that his linguisticism is perhaps most apparent. Not even *Hamlet*, in which 'word' is a dominant theme, is so charged with sensitivity to the processes and uses of language or so rich in linguistic criticism. It might not be excessive indeed to regard *Love's Labour's Lost* as being by emphasis a comedy on the English *état de langue*.

Stylistically, its characters are disposed into three social groups: a large group consisting of the courtiers and their feminine opposites, the academic trio of Armado, Nathaniel, and Holofernes, and the yokel trio of Costard, Dull, and Jaquenetta—Moth, the remaining character, is linguistically an intermediary but closest to the courtiers. Allowing for the peculiarities of poetical theatre and of employing a recent terminology, one may label the three styles U, Would-be-U, and Non-U—although they are not so distinct as that classification might suggest.

What unites the first two groups and also affects the third is an attitude towards language that may fairly be called Elizabethan. In Shakespeare's day, people who wrote books and pamphlets, and even who wrote only letters, were seemingly entranced by language: they approached it with the same speculative and playful eye that an actor turns upon his robes and paint. Some quiet, sober writers there were, of course; men who preferred to work within the limited ranges of well-established usage, but they were few in comparison with the writers who aimed at more striking styles, styles which achieved their effects by drawing upon the more recondite lexicon and semantics of the language, by patterning and playing with its phonology, by assembling its syntactic elements into uncustomary structures, by joining to their jointure of English the riches of alien tongues. From our distance, we may perhaps doubt that so formidable an exuberance was altogether typical of everyday or Everyman's usage: the devices are apt to be too *recherché*, smell too much of the book and the lamp, to be normal linguistic practice, especially the practice of speech. Nevertheless, it is the habit of much of the written English of the time, and the playwrights and others who make use of dialogue are too consistent in their linguistic plenitude to warrant a sceptic in questioning that Elizabethans, even speaking ones, were considerably more absorbed by the game of words than were their simpler forebears or their more controlled successors.

Many factors contributed to this linguistic obsession: schoolmasters, rhetoricians, schoolbooks, dictionaries, travel, translation, the doctrine of imitation, printing, the pulpit, the theatre itself—

to mention only some. But the basic drive was an idea that began in the late Middle Ages and continued well into the seventeenth century, not only in England but on the continent too—the idea that the vernaculars which had taken over the vast literary service that had once been performed by clerical Latin were inadequate to their task and needed to be augmented in all their phases, the rhetorical and semantic as well as the lexicographical and syntactic. How prevalent that notion was in Shakespeare's day may be judged by the abundant expressions of it that are assembled in Professor R. F. Jones's *Triumph of the English Language*: how prevalent was the practice of augmentation in lexicon and meaning may be seen by even a casual glance at the dates in the *O.E.D.* But repetition may represent cliché as well as conviction, and that all the augmentation was necessary is flatly denied by the record; as the *O.E.D.* shows, most of the augmentations failed to outlive the augmenters. What may be begun from a conviction of necessity may soon become fashion, and it is more than a little obvious that much of the plethora of Elizabethan English (like the plethora of Rabelais's French) was a product of form and delight rather than of impoverished necessity. One may learn much about an age from the behaviour of its heroes, and in Shakespeare's day the glass of fashion and the mould (or ape) of form was by definition a man of golden and painted words, one adept in playing pleasingly on all the strings and stops of the language.

The most obvious aspect of this plethoric style in *Love's Labour's Lost* is the lexicographical abundance that characterizes both U and Would-be-U speakers. All of them are verbal cornucopias, and sometimes they speak like Florio's dictionary, in which the words are defined by as many synonyms as the lexicographer can muster. This lexicographical manner is the special mark of the Would-be-U:

> I did converse this quondam day with a companion of the King's, who is intituled, nominated, or called Don Adriano de Armado.
>
> Novi hominem tanquam te; his humour is lofty, his discourse peremptory, his tongue filed, his eye ambitious, his gait majestical, and his general behaviour vain, ridiculous, and thrasonical.

He is too picked, too spruce, too affected, too odd, as it were, too peregrinate, as I may call it (V. i. 7 ff.).

That is Nathaniel and Holofernes, who in Moth's words 'have been at a great feast of languages and stol'n the scraps'. But the same and similar practices are shared by the courtiers—they may be found in Biron's commentary on Cupid, or in Katherine's:

> He made her melancholy, sad, and heavy;
> And so she died. Had she been light, like you,
> Of such a merry, nimble, stirring spirit
> She might 'a been a grandam ere she died (V ii. 16 ff.).

The differentiation between U and Would-be-U lies largely in example, degree, and mood. If to the King it was Armado who was the man of linguistic fashion, one whom 'the music of his own vain tongue, Doth ravish like enchanting harmony', to Biron, the ape of this particular linguistic fashion was 'honey-tongu'd Boyet', the courtier de luxe. All the speakers in fact employ words that must have seemed strange to a large part of a Globe audience—that the *O.E.D.* may now record earlier appearance is of little significance, for the Elizabethan neologist had no such dictionary in which to check the activities of his rivals and Shakespeare's audiences had only their awareness of context to lead them the right way. All of the speakers, too, are inclined to be bookish in their speech—'fair as a text B in a copy book'. But the U-speakers are less obvious, less extreme in neologism than the Would-be's, and more playful and easy in their practice. Holofernes, Nathaniel, and Armado have eaten paper; Armado is 'a man of fire-new words, fashion's own knight', Holofernes and Nathaniel are linguistically Arts-men. The courtiers exploit the language at all social levels, the courtliness of their speech is mixed with words and especially meanings that are even more familiar to the proletarians of the play. The Would-be's on the other hand, are dominated by a desire to be 'singuled from the barbarous', to differentiate themselves linguistically from the non-U's with whom they are most closely associated in society.

In so doing they ape the courtly fashion, but solemnly, excessively, absurdly, and inadequately. For although they flaunt their neologisms and grossly marry Latin with English, they lack the awareness of vulgar usage which links the courtiers to the non-U's; they are more aware of a 'most singular and choice epithet' than of the vulgar (and usually unseemly) connotations of words that they themselves use, everyday words like *limb, joint, brawl,* or *cull'd,* and even learned words of their own importing, *posterior,* for instance.

Plays, like sermons and orations, live on the boundary of writing and speech, and it is therefore to be expected that a playwright will exploit the phonology of the language more than, say, a novelist—his equipment, moreover, includes the actor's voice and gesture. So it is that *Love's Labour's Lost* exploits features of the English tongue that would be hard for a writer whose works were meant for silent readers. Pronunciation in its various social styles is every playwright's concern, and in *Love's Labour's Lost,* although there is no attempt at a complete directive, there are hints to the actor in all three classes—hints of the kind that appear in the songs written for the Cockney comedians of the later English music-halls. These spelling hints point to an easy, colloquial style of pronunciation among the courtiers—'Whoe'er 'a was, 'a show'd a mounting mind', says the Princess. Whether they also employed the tone and timbre that is now the most distinctive feature of U-speech—it is obvious even when the words and syntax cannot be distinguished—is something that can only be guessed at, though it is my own guess that part of the 'accent' in which the courtiers instructed Moth when they sent him with their verses was the accent which in the linguist's more exact term is timbre. The yokels are presented as dialect-speakers: towards the end of the play Costard is given words and pronunciations that form directives to the actor to play him as a Northerner. No such hints are given for Dull: topographical logic might suggest that he too should be played with a Northern pronunciation, but topographical logic was scarcely compelling in Shakespeare's theatre. The pedants may be held to be typified in Holofernes. Unlike the courtiers and yokels, he abhorred many a pronunciation that had been on every Englishman's tongue for generations (*det, dout, cauf, hauf, nebour* are his particular examples), preferring, and doubtless using, pronunciations promulgated by etymological pedants. *Natural: artificial* is the opposition in this area, with the U's and the non-U's joined in opposition to the Would-be's.

Alliteration, the device of assembling phonemic patterns unnatural in normal usage, is a linguistic game that the characters of *Love's Labour's Lost* share with a large proportion of the Elizabethan literary world—it is a sport as apparent on the page as on the tongue. But the courtiers differ from the pedants in the way they use it. The courtiers tend to employ the device lightly, and in the context of wit:

Study is like the heaven's glorious sun
That will not be deep-search'd with saucy looks (I. i. 84 ff.).

For Holofernes, however, it is something to be displayed in gross obviousness, and as a matter of linguistic status:

I will something affect the letter, for it argues facility. The preyful Princess pierc'd and prick'd a pretty pleasing pricket.
(IV. ii. 52 ff.)

The other phonological game that *Love's Labour's Lost* shares with Elizabethan literature in general is the pun, the device of playing upon the homophones and near-homophones of the language. If for Shakespeare (which means Shakespeare's characters too) the pun was a Cleopatra, the reason should be apparent from his dealings with the larger aspects of the language. Abundance of pronunciation doublets within good speech and the variations provided by the speech of different social levels and dialects afforded an infinite variety for both playwright and actor. It is a game that is best played orally, and the virtuoso player is the man who can best exploit the near-homonym or the most variants. In *Love's Labour's Lost*, the courtiers pun upon homonyms provided not only by good usage, *äy* and *eye* for example, but also upon equations that, according to the pronunciation manuals and the practice of Mistress Quickly, were used only by the vulgar—*shooter* and *suitor, qualm* and *calm* are cases in point. To the same comic end, they also exploit current variants in stress and juncture. Thus, the Princess achieves a witty commentary on the King's greeting simply by shifting the stress of one word— 'You shall be welcome madam' . . . 'I will be welcome then'—and Dumain plays greasily upon the semantic significance of two different stresses in *Judas*. Costard, as his confusing way with *plantain* shows, shares something of the courtiers' pleasure in phonological gamesmanship, but Holofernes is not only slow in grasping the phonological ploys of others, he is also laboriously exegetical in using them himself:

> Master Person, quasi per-son. And if one should be pierc'd, which is the one? (IV ii. 79 ff.).

In semantics, the most striking feature of the play is the fascination of almost all the characters in face of the extremes of meaning that a word may carry. The pedants are prone to express this fascination in synonymical lists. The courtiers are more subtle and varied. Everyday English usage provided them with a great many words that, in Doll Tearsheat's phrase, were excellent good words before they became ill-sorted—*yard, horn, prick,* and their like—and these are principal pieces in the courtiers' armoury of wit. But in their gay verbal battles they are busy to add to the common stock. The semantic principles of extension and association are their method, and by its means they contrive *double-entendres* for the most innocent of words—*in, out, mark, howl,* to list only a few. Costard, no fool though a clown, can admire this gay facility in perverting linguistic process:

> O' my troth, most sweet jests! most incony vulgar wit!
> When it comes so smoothly off, so obscenely, as it were, so fit!
> (IV. i. 135 ff.)

but, as the colloquy between Holofernes, Nathaniel and Dull on *pricket* and *haud credo* shows, similar wit in the pedants and yokels is apt to be accidental rather than deliberate, the playwright's rather than their own.

Falstaff's disquisition on apoplexy may be Shakespeare's most extended example of wit joined to semantic principle—as the reader may remember, the word is brought by many shifts to mean deafness. But *Love's Labour's Lost* affords examples no less complex, as when Biron plays shuttlecock with the many meanings of *light*; or when Armado, with assists (*anglice*, help) from Moth and Costard, manages to confuse *plantains, gesse, envoys*, and two sorts of *salve* into proximate meaning; or again, when by perverse associationism ('sympathizing' as it is termed), *lead, rhetoric, smoke, bullet, cannon* are gallimaufried into a single pot of meaning.

Most of this essay has dealt with the U's and Would-be's. The Non-U's are not without linguistic interest, however. At bottom they are countrymen, speakers of dialect, users of plain, traditional English. But they are not immune from linguistic fashion either. Jacquenetta is the character of least words, and it may not be insignificant that she is also the woman of speediest action; she is two months gone when the court-ladies have a year and more to go. Dull, whose taciturnity in the midst of general loquacity reminds one of Silence in the company of Shallow and Falstaff, is in a way an ironical yardstick. Yokel though he is, 'a twice-sod simplicity, *bis coctus*,' under the pressure of the law and the Arts-men he is nevertheless prone to be seduced from his usual plain speech into learned malapropisms whose wit is none of his own intending (the learned *allusion*, for example, which on his simple tongue is transformed into *collusion* and *pollusion*). Costard, who is a half-way figure, a clown in two senses, is occasionally unconsciously witty in Dull's way though the ground of his speech is sound enough. But he has much of the court manner, too; he is adroit and persistent in puns, he can deliberately tangle a word with a bogus etymology, and in semantic juggling with several balls he is almost as skilful as Biron:

In manner and form following, sir; all those three: I was seen with her in the manor-house, sitting with her upon the form, and taken following her into the park; which, put together, is in manner and form following. Now, sir, for the manner—it is the manner of a man to speak to a woman. For the form—in some form (I. i. 201 ff.).

Pondering on the language of the rustics, a solemn critic might even come to think that one of Shakespeare's intentions in *Love's Labour's Lost* was to show how city fashion can linguistically corrupt country simplicity and directness.

Embodied and on stage, *Love's Labour's Lost* can seem a thing of elegant pattern and dancing grace; a ballet of fireflies, as it were. On the page, its tensions are more strained: a delicate reader may think he is attending a Mad Linguists' Party, a brilliant and amusing affair, but strangely narcissistic. Entrancing as the play may be to anyone who is himself touched with its trouble, the compulsiveness of the play's logosophy may still strike him as somewhat neurotic. To others, such an impression may seem anachronistic and certainly over-solemn. But that it is not altogether *malapropos*, and even that linguistic disease may be an intended motif of the play, may be supported by some Elizabethan opinions on Elizabethan linguistic fashions, and by Shakespeare's own words.

Punctuating Elizabethan demands for augmenting the language, varying the eulogies on its ever-growing copiousness, is a mutter of protest that grows louder as the Elizabethan Age passes into the Jacobean. The essence of the protest is that contemporary fascination with language and its processes is a disease, a moral and intellectual disease; that what is an instrument has been made an end in itself. As early as 1570, for instance, Thomas Browne complained of his contemporaries' preference for 'painted words and smooth Rhetoricke' over 'matter good and precious'; some years later, Sir William Cornwallis speaks of their 'disease of words'; Bacon is vehement in asserting that the 'first distemper of learning' begins 'when men study words and not matter' and the title of one of Montaigne's most potent essays is, 'Of the Vanitie of Words'.[1] Shakespeare, throughout his poems and plays, bombards his audience with comments to the like effect, so

---

[1] These citations are taken from Paul Jorgensen's *Redeeming Shakespeare's Words* (1962). There are many more comments to the same effect.

abundant that they must represent his own opinion as well as that of his puppets.

It is hardly surprising that in *Love's Labour's Lost* this contrast of painted words and empty matter should be directed towards Armado: 'He draweth out the thread of his verbosity finer than the staple of his argument'—though it is rather unlooked-for that one of his critics should be Holofernes, who has his own extensive means for learnedly saying nothing at inordinate length (including Shallow's shallow trick of simple repetition). But the courtiers say very much the same about their own linguistic practice. 'Much in the letters, nothing in the praise,' says Rosaline of Biron's letter. Biron comments on the ladies' habit of slicing meanings into the thinnest of nonsense:

> The tongues of mocking wenches are as keen
> As is the razor's edge invisible,
> Cutting a smaller hair than may be seen,
> Above the sense of sense (V. ii. 256 ff.).

In the concluding armistice, the Princess can credit the courtiers' best verbal efforts (bombast and lining to the time) with the worthy motives of a pastime, but her complaisance still carries the sting of Hamlet's embittered 'Words, words, words'.

Love's Labour's Lost is a comedy on books and behaviour, words and matter, and its resolution may be a proposal for therapy. The King is sent into silence for a year; Biron is commanded to speak with the speechless and to apply his witty loquacity to a charitable end. Plain speech becomes the battle-cry. 'Honest plain words best pierce the ear of grief,' says Biron. 'Now to plain-dealing, lay these glozes by,' says Longaville. Dull triumphs over Holofernes. And Biron's resolution seeks a cure for linguistic disease in a plain and country-style of speaking:

> O, never will I trust to speeches penn'd
>   Nor to the motion of a school-boy's tongue,
> Nor never come in vizard to my friend,
>   Nor woo in rhyme, like a blind harper's song.
> Taffeta phrases, silken terms precise,

Three-pil'd hyperboles, spruce affectation,
Figures pedantical—these summer-flies
   Have blown me full of maggot ostentation.
I do foreswear them, and I here protest,
   By this white glove—how white the hand, God knows—
Henceforth my wooing mind shall be express'd
   In russet yeas, and honest kersey noes (V. ii. 402 ff.).

II

'Coriolanus': Violentest Contrariety

R. F. HILL

SHAKESPEARE'S version of the Fable of the Belly in *Coriolanus* is thought to be partly indebted to that of William Averell in *A Mervailous Combat of Contrarieties* (1588).[1] It is a curious truth that this title would aptly serve as a sub-title to *Coriolanus*. Menenius describes the quality of the opposition between Coriolanus and Aufidius as 'violentest contrariety' and the play is built upon a series of contrarieties, both moral and physical. Patricians are opposed to plebeians; Coriolanus sometimes stands alone against the plebeians, and he is during parts of the action opposed to Aufidius, Volumnia and to Rome itself. Centred in Coriolanus himself there is a knot of moral conflicts: pride desirous of merited recognition yet impatient of praise, and pride in conflict with filial duty; honesty and honour set against 'policy', and honour against mercy. The plebeians themselves are characterized by a kind of ambiguity, a vacillation between extremes of opinion and action. These contrarieties are wrought to a pitch of emotion both marvellous (i.e. exciting astonishment) and violent; they are also coloured by a strain of perversity.[2] Where, in a Shakespearian play, the issues and emotional climate are so sharply defined and homogeneous one would expect a clear correlation in its style. So far as concerns imagery such correlation has been explored; commentators have related dominant image groups of the body and disease, of animal contrasts, to the themes of political sickness and conflict.[3] Wilson Knight placed a significant emphasis on the

[1] K. Muir, *Shakespeare's Sources I* (1957), p. 224.

[2] The idea of 'contrariness', 'perversity', is suggested by 'contrariety' for the modern reader; but this sense is not cited by the *O.E.D.* until 1866.

[3] Cf. G. Wilson Knight, *The Imperial Theme* (1931), pp. 154-98; Caroline Spurgeon, *Shakespeare's Imagery* (1935), pp. 347-9; W. H. Clemen, *The Development of Shakespeare's Imagery* (1951), pp. 154-8; Maurice Charney, *Shakespeare's Roman Plays* (1961), pp. 157-69.

'violent, metallic, impactuous' nature of the imagery. Otherwise, such comments on the style of the play that I have seen have been limited to rather general observations: 'The play's style is bare . . . ice-cold, intellectual',[1] 'harshness and stridency, and ever the inevitable economy',[2] 'The verse of this play has strength and sinewiness . . . but its range of tone and feeling is unusually narrow for Shakespeare',[3] 'The style of *Coriolanus* is not so much "Roman", implying as this does a Stoic self-control, as objective and public.'[4] These criticisms are not cited in disparagement since each has its relevance, and each was made within the control of thematic considerations, but none comes to grips with the syntactical and rhetorical ordering.

Examination of such ordering of thought and verbal patterns in *Coriolanus* shows it to be pervasively antithetical and balanced. This rhetorical shaping is, of course, common to much Elizabethan prose and verse, fulfilling, in part, the grand endeavour to render English 'finely framed, and strongly trussed up together'.[5] It was fully absorbed into Shakespeare's technique, defining expression throughout his plays in the service of wit and of deeper purposes. Critics have commented on the high incidence of forms of antithesis in *Macbeth* and *King Lear* as the correlative of the plays' preoccupations with appearance and reality, with a world of ambiguity.[6] However, the means and ends of these tragedies are more complex than those of *Coriolanus*, and simple antithesis is woven into a subtle fabric of equivocation, paradox and enigma. *Coriolanus* is intense but narrow in its moral reference, and its pervasive antithesis correspondingly simpler in kind, and different in effect. It defines the nature of the contrarieties already

[1] Knight, *op. cit.*, p. 155.

[2] B. Ifor Evans, *The Language of Shakespeare's Plays* (1952), p. 174.

[3] D. J. Enright, '*Coriolanus*: Tragedy or Debate?' *Essays in Criticism*, IV (January, 1954), p. 4.

[4] Charney, *op. cit.*, p. 38.

[5] E. K.'s Prefatory Epistle to *The Shepheardes Calendar*.

[6] See, for example, *Shakespeare Jahrbuch*, Band 90 (1954), K. Muir, 'Shakespeare and Rhetoric', pp. 49–68, and Margaret D. Burrell, '*Macbeth*: A Study in Paradox', pp. 167–90.

referred to and enforces the inevitability of the violent catastrophe.

The First Citizen, as spokesman of the plebeians, voices the complaint against the patricians:

> We are accounted poor citizens, the patricians good. What authority surfeits on would relieve us; if they would yield us but the superfluity while it were wholesome, we might guess they relieved us humanely; but they think we are too dear. The leanness that afflicts us, the object of our misery, is as an inventory to particularize their abundance; our sufferance is a gain to them (I. i. 14–22).

Antithesis also characterizes his reiterated accusations at ll. 76–84. When he mingles threats the same structure persists:

> Let us revenge this with our pikes ere we become rakes (I. i. 22–3).

> They say poor suitors have strong breaths; they shall know we have strong arms too (I. i. 57–8).

When in this scene the citizens consider the character of Coriolanus they see him in terms of the contradictions which are to prove his undoing. As to Coriolanus' services to his country, the First Citizen 'could be content to give him good report for't but that he pays himself with being proud' (30–32) and 'though soft-conscienc'd men can be content to say it was for his country, he did it to please his mother' (35–8). The Second Citizen's attempt at a defence of Coriolanus, 'What he cannot help in his nature you account a vice in him' (39–40), emphasizes by antithesis the nub of the problem; that Coriolanus *cannot* modify these aspects of his nature, and that the plebeians *will* account them as vice.

In Acts II and III a succession of antithetical propositions conveys the uncompromising plebeian view of Coriolanus as they sketch him in ruthless paradox and contradiction:

> He's poor in no one fault, but stor'd with all (II. i. 16).

> O, he would miss it rather
> Than carry it but by the suit of the gentry to him
> And the desire of the nobles (II. i. 227-9).

You have deserved nobly of your country, and you have not deserved nobly (II. iii. 85-6).

> With a proud heart he wore
> His humble weeds (II. iii. 149-50).

> You speak o' th' people
> As if you were a god, to punish; not
> A man of their infirmity (III. i. 80-2).

Even where this plebeian view is mitigated by a sense of obligations due to Coriolanus' services to Rome, the statements remain inside the inflexible bonds of antithesis, so that the tension of unresolvable conflict is hardly lessened. Thus, when the Third Citizen expounds on the gratitude which ought to enforce their voices for Coriolanus (II. iii. 4-15) his arguments are strung up so tight by antithesis as to seem enforced by the situation rather than freely felt. So that, although he has admitted that recompense is necessarily due to Coriolanus, one is not surprised by the ominous offence taken a little later by the plebeians when Coriolanus asserts that his 'own desert' has brought him to the consulship. The discussion of the situation by the two officers (II. ii) is more objective but, owing to its rigid antithetical structure, again encourages little hope of a resolution of the conflicting issues.

The plebeian view of Coriolanus, conceived in terms of hated contradictions, is answered by one of a parallel nature from Coriolanus. His contempt for the plebeians leads him to characterize them in simple, reiterated extremes:

> What would you have, you curs,
> That like not peace nor war? The one affrights you,
> The other makes you proud . . .
>   . . . Who deserves greatness
> Deserves your hate . . .

> ... Hang ye! Trust ye?
> With every minute you do change a mind
> And call him noble that was now your hate,
> Him vile that was your garland (I. i. 166–82).

> You souls of geese
> That bear the shapes of men, how have you run
> From slaves that apes would beat! (I. iv. 34–6).

> Must these have voices, that can yield them now
> And straight disclaim their tongues? (III. i. 34–5).

Coriolanus' admonition to senators and patricians concerning the balance of power in Rome (III. i. 64–170) is wholly cast in sharp antitheses of thought and verbal structure, thus heightening our apprehension of a fearful issue. In the confusion which follows, the arguments between plebeians and patricians are taut to breaking point as antithetical threats and assertions are bandied to and fro. (Cf. ll. 197, 198, 204–7, 218–20, 220–2, 238–40, 248–50, 275–6.) The last part of this scene centres the problem exactly about Coriolanus, and when with customary rhetorical balance Menenius characterizes him,

> His heart's his mouth;
> What his breast forges, that his tongue must vent; (III. i. 257–8).

he announces the theme of the next scene, the conflict of honour and policy which will lacerate the heart of Coriolanus and divide him from kith and country.

Coriolanus listens astounded to the dictates of his mother, that he should return to the plebeians, repentant, lying, flattering, a course of action at flat variance with the 'nobility' she has fostered in him. The incompatibility of such a course with his sense of honour shapes itself in unresolvable antitheses:

> Would you have me
> False to my nature? Rather say I play
> The man I am (III. ii. 14–16).

> I cannot do it to the gods;
> Must I then do't to them? (III. ii. 38-9).

> Must I
> With my base tongue give to my noble heart
> A lie that it must bear? (III. ii. 99-101).

Only by the insistence of Volumnia can he be brought to *attempt* the part, when the rebuke of filial disobedience touches the Achilles' heel of his massive will. His honour must submit to the honour due to her, here as later at the gates of Rome, and we glimpse momentarily that hidden conflict in his nature which is caught in Aufidius' cruel but shrewd taunt, 'thou boy of tears.'[1] Volumnia probes this conflict in a series of antitheses at III. ii. 23-30, while earlier in the scene she has struck out other contrarieties:

> You might have been enough the man you are
> With striving to be less so (19-20).

> I know though hadst rather
> Follow thine enemy in a fiery gulf
> Than flatter him in a bower (90-92).

> I have a heart as little apt as yours,
> But yet a brain that leads my use of anger
> To better vantage (29-31).

Coriolanus is not in fact deficient in intelligence, as he demonstrates in his clear-sighted and well-marshalled address to the patricians (III. i. 90-112). But his intelligence is not of the order that can persuade him to compromise his honour.

That is one strand in his pride; another is that consciousness of worth which is inverted to issue as extravagant false humility. The very extravagance ought to alert us as to the probable complexity of the impulse. And, on examination, while it is clear that

---

[1] See I. R. Browning, *'Coriolanus*: Boy of Tears', *Essays in Criticism*, V (January, 1955), pp. 18-31.

Coriolanus is incapable of true humility, it is equally clear that his wilfulness in deprecating his achievements is exacerbated by that other facet of his pride, an integrity contemptuous of flattery and double-dealing. The strength of conflicting feelings in him fitly expresses itself in exaggerated oppositions. Thus he rejects the just praise for his deeds at Corioli:

> Pray now, no more; my mother,
> Who has a charter to extol her blood,
> When she does praise me grieves me (I. ix. 13–15).

> I thank you, General,
> But cannot make my heart consent to take
> A bribe to pay my sword (III. ix. 36–8).

So also upon his return to Rome:

> I had rather have my wounds to heal again
> Than hear say how I got them (II. ii. 67–8).

> I had rather have one scratch my head i' th' sun
> When the alarum were struck than idly sit
> To hear my nothings monster'd (II. ii. 73–5).

The conflict inside Coriolanus sets up a problem for his associates which they are incapable of resolving since their attitudes to both Coriolanus and the plebeians are rendered immovable by class prejudice. They can only, on the one hand, urge him to dissimulate and, on the other, plead his soldier-like bluntness to the plebeians and insist upon Rome's debt to his services.

Consideration of the fixed attitudes of the patricians is a reminder that those of Coriolanus and the plebeians are equally so. Thus the action of the play presents itself not simply as a study of conflicts but of intransigence. From this intransigence the tragedy stems, for where no concession or compromise is possible a violent catastrophe must follow. It has already been shown how the conflicts determine the persistent antithesis in *Coriolanus*; by the same means the intransigence is caught and conveyed to us. For the antithesis continually sets ideas at the extreme of variance, at hyperbolical stretch, thereby intimating violence of attitude, and gradually impressing upon us the impossibility of reconciliation. Violent, unthinking opinion leads through antithesis to crude over-simplifications and self-deceptions. Thus crudely Coriolanus views the plebeians: in war they are frightened, in peace they are proud; they are not lions but hares, not foxes but geese; the man who deserves greatness deserves their hate. Brutus, the tribune, sees Coriolanus as 'poor in no one fault, but stor'd with all'; to Sicinius he is one who 'would depopulate the city and Be every man himself'. The loud-mouthed First Citizen evaluates with similar crudity and exaggeration: 'What authority surfeits on would relieve us', 'Let us revenge this with our pikes ere we become rakes.'

As one tracks the antitheses through the play one is horrified by the crudeness and immoderation which flaw the principal characters, by their inadequacy in human relationships. Even Menenius has only a veneer of wit and policy. In the first scene of the play he attempts to reason with the plebeians, but his lip curls at the First Citizen and the fangs of his prejudice are bared in his onslaught on the Tribunes (II. i.): 'a very little thief of occasion will rob you of a great deal of patience . . . I know you can do very little alone; for your helps are many . . . and though I must be content to bear with those that say you are reverend grave men, yet they lie deadly that tell you you have good faces.' The quality of this wit places Menenius, at bottom, in the same category as the plebeians, Coriolanus and Volumnia; ever the crude simplifications, evaluations and hyperbolical antitheses. Thus, Menenius of Coriolanus' letter:

The most sovereign prescription in Galen is but empiricutic and, to this preservative, of no better report than a horse-drench (II. i. 8–10).

Volumnia, on war and honour:

If my son were my husband, I should freelier rejoice in that

absence wherein he won honour than in the embracements of
his bed where he would show most love . . .

. . . I had rather had eleven [sons] die nobly for their country
than one voluptuously surfeit out of action (I. ii. 2–25).

The unbending nature of the passions and opinions of Coriolanus
himself has been sufficiently illustrated; we need only remind
ourselves here that his intransigence embraces not only his opposition to the plebeians but also the conflicts within himself.

Intransigence, then, is the governing character of the opposing
forces in *Coriolanus*. I have suggested—necessarily somewhat
briefly—that this intransigence springs from class prejudice and an
inadequacy of the moral imagination. It follows that no mutual
understanding or true rapprochement is possible, and that intransigence can only be modified at the dictates of pure self-
interest—policy and necessity. This is precisely true of both
plebeians and patricians. When the settled hatred of the tribunes
for Coriolanus has contrived the revocation of the plebeian
'voices' and thus precipitated the central crisis of the play, the
patricians do not, as they should by virtue of their moral responsi-
bility as guardians of the state, attempt to mediate by a mature
consideration of the rights and wrongs of the incensed parties.
Their former attitude to the plebeians and to Coriolanus remains
unexamined, and their sole impulse is to temporize—'this must be
patch'd With cloth of any colour' (III. i. 253–4). In the same
scene, Menenius still considers that the rage of Coriolanus is
'worthy', and, in answer to the bald statement of the First Patri-
cian that 'This man has marr'd his fortune', Menenius merely
reiterates his nobility, his inability to flatter or mask his feelings.
In the next scene (III. ii) the patricians persist in their crude
evaluation of the plebeians—they are 'the herd', 'our general
louts', 'the ignorant', and their only censure of Coriolanus is for
his impolitic rashness. They are incapable of enriching his con-
cept of honour by showing its compatibility with humility, for-
giveness, patience, compassion, imaginative understanding.
Volumnia applauds the 'honour' she has cultivated in him, and

asks only that his obsidian class-hatred be dissimulated in the interests of policy. This is the measure of her political and ethical stature as it is, indeed, of the play as a whole. Critics have noted the poetical leanness of *Coriolanus*; the leanness is moral and, consequently, poetical.

The intransigence of the plebeians—at least in so far as it is fostered by the tribunes—submits only to necessity. They hoot Coriolanus out of the city in the character of the 'people's enemy' but, upon the threat of a vengeful return, they are driven by fear to excuse their ill-considered action—'I ever said we were i' th' wrong when we banish'd him' (IV. vi. 155–6). The panic-stricken tribunes fawn upon the patricians, paradoxically appealing to a humanity in Coriolanus which in their triumphant hatred they had denied him; so Brutus pleads to Menenius, 'You know the very way into his kindness' (V. i. 59). And when Volumnia prevails, she and her family are hailed into the city with blessings.

Where does Coriolanus himself stand, morally, in this study of intransigence? Surely incomparably higher than all? It is all too evident that his mother is to blame for the narrowness of his vision, while the element of perversity in his pride can be tracked to a revulsion from flattery and related duplicities. But his clear superiority stands in his incapacity to sacrifice his integrity to political expediency. His two attempts, at the extreme urging of the patricians and his mother, are in reality still-born. The impossibility of the situation for Coriolanus is expressed in his clear-sighted and tragically loaded antithesis:

> Know, good mother,
> I had rather be their servant in my way
> Than sway with them in theirs (II. i. 192–4).

The action unrolls its fated course until the supreme test is exacted upon Coriolanus, in which he substantiates his claim to nobility and attains tragic stature.[1] For *his* intransigence bows finally to

[1] Sailendra Kumar Sen ['What Happens in *Coriolanus*', *Shakespeare Quarterly*, IX (Summer, 1958), pp. 331–45] emphasizes the inward conflict suffered by Coriolanus, and shows it to be essential to his tragic stature. This inward conflict was Shakespeare's pointing up of Plutarch's account.

mercy and the bond of nature, with an act which is at once an immolation of his pride and of his life:

> O my mother, mother! O!
> You have won a happy victory to Rome;
> But for your son—believe it, O, believe it!—
> Most dangerously you have with him prevail'd,
> If not most mortal to him. But let it come (V. iii. 185–9).

Most mortal, indeed, for Aufidius is waiting, eager to accomplish the destruction of the ruin left by plebeians and patricians—Aufidius, whose 'intransigence', his hatred of Coriolanus, could temporize like theirs when expediency required:

> I am glad thou has set thy mercy and thy honour
> At difference in thee. Out of that I'll work
> Myself a former fortune (V. iii. 200–202).

To ennoble Coriolanus unreservedly would be foolish and I have only sought to show how a moral superiority is established over a deeply flawed society. His intransigence is a compound of folly and integrity and as such proceeds to both failure and nobility. His outraged pride and sense of injured merit drive him to an act that appals. He is, indeed, 'a god to punish, in the enormity of his wrath.' Menenius is incredulous of the news of Coriolanus' pact:

> This is unlikely.
> He and Aufidius can no more atone
> Than violent'st contrariety (IV. vi. 72–4).

This atoning of violentest contrariety measures not only the fearfulness of the intransigence but also the criminal folly of the society from which it sprang. They had lived by violent contrarieties, and where reason, tolerance, understanding could never work to a rapprochement of opposites, there would one day come an 'atoning' of violence. Coriolanus and Aufidius atone in one sense, and in another all Rome must atone.

This brief study of antithesis in *Coriolanus* has sought to illustrate the close correlation between poetic means and imaginative prehensions. Where such correlation obtains analysis of means leads naturally into interpretation. My interpretative statement is admittedly a simplification of detail (I am aware, for example, that I have not been fair to a latent generous impulse in the plebeians, stifled by the demagogue tribunes) but I am convinced of its centrality. It is certainly consonant with the play's imagery, characterized by critics as 'violent, metallic, impactuous' and as consisting in extreme contrasts. As to whether the play is a tragedy or debate, a problem canvassed by D. J. Enright[1] and answered by I. R. Browning,[2] my findings suggest tragedy. The antithesis only superficially suggests the thrust and parry of debate. for there is no proper engagement or analysis of thought, but only a blank facing of entrenched positions. The antithesis, shaping thought into violent oppositions, conveys this intransigence. That the play is 'thin' is not due to some quality of intellectual debate; it is the moral indictment of a society.

[1] *Essays in Criticism*, loc. cit.
[2] *Essays in Criticism*, loc. cit.

III

The Lost 'Troilus and Cressida'

G. BULLOUGH

WE shall never know what made Shakespeare write some of his plays, but it is interesting to speculate on possibilities. Was 1 *Henry VI* inspired by the French wars of 1589–92? *A Midsummer Night's Dream* by the wedding of an elderly nobleman flattered to be compared with Theseus? *Did* Queen Elizabeth demand a play on 'Falstaff in love' and get *The Merry Wives of Windsor?* Doubtless Shakespeare was encouraged by many factors: stage fashion, rivalry with other companies, a desire to break new ground, his own pleasure in particular themes found in short stories, romances and older plays.

Shakespeare's *Troilus and Cressida* affords many puzzles. Was it the fruit of amorous despair or moral disgust at current tendencies in English society, or of fear that the Queen's death might bring a descent into the disorder recently averted? For the play, probably written and performed in 1602, was entered in the Stationers' Register to 'Master Roberts, as it is acted by my lord Chamberlain's Men'. Was it written to mock at Chapman's *Homer* (Chapman being perhaps the 'Rival Poet' of the *Sonnets*) or to counter Jonson's worship of the classics? These and many other suggestions have been made to explain the peculiar satiric bitterness of *Troilus and Cressida*. They may all be true, but nothing can be proved with certainty. Some light may be cast on Shakespeare's intentions and achievement if we consider a lost play on the Troy theme, of which some fragmentary indications survive.

There were several plays on the Siege of Troy and persons connected with it before Shakespeare wrote. A translation of Seneca's *Agamemnon* was printed in 1566 and again in 1581, and Oxford's Boys had played an *Agamemnon and Ulysses* at Court on 27

December 1584. An *Ajax and Ulysses* (probably based on Ovid) was done by Windsor Chapel boys on 1 January 1572. Henslowe's *Diary* contains several references to Troy plays. In June and July 1596 a new play called *Troy* was performed by the Admiral's Men—who possessed 'a great horse' probably suitable for such a piece. In February 1599 Henslowe paid 'Harey Cheattell' for 'a play called Troyes Revenge with the tragedy of Polefcme'. In April he paid 'Mr. dickers and harey Chcattell' for a *Troyelles & Cresseda*. (The same title also appears above entries for January 1594, but Greg thought the writing was not Henslowe's.) A month later, on 26 and 30 May 1599, Dekker and Chettle were paid £4 15s. od. for 'the tragedie of Agamemnon' which was to be licensed in June 1599.

So the Admiral's Men had three plays, a *Troy*, a *Troilus and Cressida*, and an *Agamemnon*, which together may have covered the Troy story from the start of the siege to Agamemnon's murder, and a fourth play on the misadventures of Ulysses on his way home.

A manuscript volume in the British Museum (Add. MSS. 10,449) contains the 'plots', or prompter's and call-boy's outlines, of five plays produced by Henslowe's company, the Admiral's Men. One of these 'plots', though sadly mutilated, clearly belongs to a *Troilus and Cressida* play, and Sir W. W. Greg, who transcribed it,[1] considered that it had to do with the *Troilus and Cressida* written by Thomas Dekker and Henry Chettle in April 1599, rather than with the *Troy* play of 1596, since it contains the names of several actors who belonged to the company between 1597 and February 1602.[2] I propose to consider the possible contents of the play concerned, and its relationship to Shakespeare's *Troilus*, written within three years afterwards.

The 'Admiral's Plot' is written in two columns on part of a single sheet of paper mounted on pasteboard in modern times.

---

[1] Cf. W. W. Greg, *Henslowe Papers* (1907), p. 142; *Dramatic Documents from the Elizabethan Playhouses* (1931), pp. 138–43; *Variorum TC*, p. 459–61.

[2] I.e. Thomas Hunt, Richard Jones, Stephen (? Maget) and two boy actors, 'Mr. Jones his boy' and John Pigg or Pyk. Cf. *Henslowe's Diary*, ed. R. A. Foakes and R. T. Rickert (Cambridge 1961), p. 329.

Probably intended to be hung up behind the stage, it covers thirteen scenes, and gives entrances, exits, stage effects, the names of characters, and some actors. Greg considered it to be 'roughly the lower half of the front or first sheet' which was 'apparently continued on the back'. J. S. P. Tatlock[1] believed that 'there is probably not a very large amount lost'. But whereas other extant plots measure between 16 and 18 inches deep (*The Honest Man's Fortune* 16.5 and *The Battle of Alcazar* 18 inches), the fragment is only $7\frac{1}{2}$ inches at deepest and less than 5 inches at its narrowest. Since more than the top half of the 'Plot' is wanting and the bottom portion has six scenes on the left and seven on the right it may be that the first half-dozen scenes and as many in the middle are missing. The extant portion of the Plot then represents part of the second and fourth quarters of the play, or (if the end of the piece was on another side) the second and fourth fifths of the whole. The following survey is greatly indebted to the brief analysis by J. S. P. Tatlock[2] who because of the form 'Menalay' believed that the author drew mainly on Lydgate's *Troy-Book* (perhaps also on Caxton's *Recuyell of the Historyes of Troye*) for his material; 'yet an acquaintance with Homer is apparent, especially in scene 10 (J). Chaucer's *Troilus and Criseyde* underlies the figure of Pandarus and the loves of Troilus and Cressida, and Henryson's *Testament of Cresseid* her punishment'.

A reproduction of the torn, faded text in BM. MS. 10,449 is given in the plate facing page 38. I have tried below to reconstruct the 'Plot' and the probable material of the play scene by scene. My textual readings owe much to Greg's reconstruction in *Dramatic Documents*, Plate V, but differ in some details, and I have been less rigorous, since in placing within brackets probable readings of the fragmentary text I have included some letters not actually visible in the original. I use his alphabetical method of enumerating scenes. The words in the left-hand column refer to stage-effects, noises 'off', trumpets, etc.

[1] 'The Siege of Troy in Shakespeare and Heywood.' *PMLA*. xxx. (New Ser. xxiii) 1915.

[2] op. cit. pp. 697–703.

Scene A

            (Ente)r at . . .
            (   )reo( )e,
            Ulisses   A(ia)x
            dore (He)rrauld
            (Pr)iam, Hecto(r), (D)eiph(obus)
            (ex)eunt (to) *crossed out* (Dio)med,
            & (D)eiphob(us)   the rest &
            (Herr)a(u)lds, to (the)m Menalaus
3. severa(ll)   (Ulisse?)s & Diomede, to them Hector
(T)ucketts   (Deip)hobus, to them Cassandra   exeunt.

This conference scene is probably set at Troy, in Priam's palace. Lydgate and Caxton have two such scenes. At the beginning of the Troy story the Greeks have seized Hesione, Priam's sister and will not free her when Antenor is sent to get her back (*Troy Book*, Bk. II, 2063–2304). Priam consults his sons about avenging this injury and Paris proposes an expedition to raid the islands and seize a Greek hostage. Deiphobus supports him (*TB*. II. 2840–2899; *C*. pp. 522–3),[1] but Helenus warns them against it (*TB*. 2900–2988). Then Troilus calls his brother 'a coward priest' (cf. Shakespeare, II. ii. 37–45) and bids them seek revenge. Later Pentheus is scolded for siding with Helenus, and Cassandra prophesies woe but appeals to Priam in vain (*TB*. 3225–3279). After this Paris seizes Helen on the island of Cythera.

Since Scene A includes Greeks as well as Trojans it probably refers to a later incident when Agamemnon advises the Greeks to recover Helen peacefully if possible, and 'they cheese for they messangers Dyomedes and Ulixes for to goo to Troye and make theyr legacion' (*C*. 558–9). They find Priam sitting in his wonderful palace among his lords and enter rudely 'with sterne cheere and froward countenaunce' (*TB*. II. 6809). Ulysses demands the return of Helen to Menelaus, with compensation for Paris's misdeeds. Priam recites his wrongs. He would kill Ulysses for his discourtesy if he were not an ambassador, and orders him to leave (*TB*. II. 6950–56). When Diomed replies roughly

[1] References are to *Troy Book* [*T.B.*] ed. H. Bergen, E.E.T.S., 4 vols., 1906–12, and to *Recuyell of the Historyes of Troye*, ed. H.O. Sommer, 1894, Vol. II (*C*).

Ther rose up some be the kynges syde
With swerdis drawe, and on hym han falle
And al to hew, ther amonge hem alle . . .

Priam restrains his lords (*TB*. II. 7000–14). Aeneas and Diomed speak despitefully to one another and the Greeks leave to give the Trojans' answer to Agamemnon.

Scene A may take place in the palace of Priam, but the various exits and the coming of Menelaus may indicate a scene outside the walls where both camps may be seen. '( )reo( )e' in line 2 may be Mereone (Meryon), a king of Crete, who in Lydgate prevents Hector from spoiling Patroclus's corpse and is later killed by Hector (III. 812–18, 1889–1905). Perhaps the killing of Patroclus and Mereone's part were enacted in one of the play's missing scenes; more probably Patroclus's death was only narrated by Ajax in Scene J. Ajax is a member of the Greek embassy because he is important later. With Ulysses (and Diomed?) he is announced by the Heralds. They confront Priam, Hector and Deiphobus.

No doubt the return of the captured women is refused. Priam and his sons retire. The movements of Deiphobus are obscure, but maybe he and Diomed quarrel and go out. Menelaus probably demands his wife. The re-entry of Hector with Deiphobus may be to challenge the Greek champions, and Cassandra no doubt foretells the destruction of Troy (*TB*. II. 3225–3318) and possibly the end of Hector. The '3 severall Tucketts' would sound to introduce the Ambassadors, Priam, and Menelaus respectively.

If the scene mingles material from both conference scenes in the medieval sources it may be that the Trojan leaders discuss the advisability of returning Helen, as in Shakespeare II.ii., and that Hector is for letting Helen go while Deiphobus is for keeping her. Cassandra's exit may precede that of the others, as in Shakespeare; theirs is not noted.

The next scene is introduced by 'Excursions', i.e. men running about the stage and fighting.

Scene B
  Alaru(m)   Excursions
  excursions   Enter Hector & (Antenor *crossed out*) Priam:
                                                Mr. Jones exeunt.

The war is in full fury, and doubtless Hector and his father reveal what has been happening. The scene may mark the opening of the great battle when Hector tells Priam his plan (*TB*. Bk. III. 395–535) and requests him to hold the city's rear with reinforcements while he attacks in the front. Priam wholly trusts his son and prays the gods to make him victorious. In Lydgate the Trojan ladies, including Helen and Polyxena, mount the walls to watch the battle.

More probably the scene may show Priam bringing reinforcements to Hector's aid when the latter is hard-pressed (*TB*. III. 1960–85). In that case Hector would tell how Troilus and Ulysses wounded each other and he himself was wounded. Father and son go out and defeat the Greeks. Hector fights Ajax but forbears because they are kinsmen, and by ceasing to pursue the fleeing enemy seals the fate of Troy.

Scene C
  exc(ursions)   Enter A(   )

This may be the combat between Ajax and Hector (*TB*. 1950–2151). But the appearance of Achilles refusing to fight would contrast effectively with Scene B.

Scene D
  Alarum   (En)ter Antenor pursue(d) by Diomede
               to them Ajax, to th(em) on the
               walls Hector Paris (&) Deiphobus
  (R)etr(ea)t   & (M)r H(u)nt   exeunt.

In this scene 'Antenor is evidently captured' (Tatlock). Caxton tells (600) how, after Diomed killed the 'dreadful Sagittary' (mentioned by Shakespeare, V. v. 14–15), 'at this medle was

Anthenor taken and sente to their tentes notwithstandyng that
Polidamus his sone dyde mervaylles of armes for to resscowe
hym, but he myght not'. Lydgate used almost the same terms
(III. 3549–59). Neither named Antenor's captors but the dramatist attributes his defeat to Greeks important in his scheme. By
placing the Trojan princes on the walls the incident is made
important, as it is, since in Chaucer (and Shakespeare) the
exchange of Antenor later separates Troilus and Cressida (and
Antenor, overcome by Greek wiles, became a defeatist and helped
to betray Troy). (Did 'Mr. Hunt' play Prince Helenus?) Shakespeare does not show the capture of Antenor, though he refers to
it (III. iii. 18–19). Perhaps Hector issues his challenge to the
Greeks in this scene of the Plot.

Since the capture of Antenor is of great moment to Troilus and
Cressida the next scene shows them together. Neither Lydgate
nor Caxton wrote much of their love, but Lydgate described their
sorrow at parting (*TB*. III. 4077–4236) and both referred to
Chaucer's poem for further details. The dramatist therefore turns
to *Troilus and Criseyde* for his fifth scene:

Scene E.

> Enter Tro(y)l(u)s & Pandarus
> to t(h)em Cressida & a waight (ing)
> maid wth a l(ig)ht, Mr. Jones his boy
> exit (w)ai(g)hting maid, exeunt manet
> Pan(darus) to (h)im Deiphobus, exit
> D(ei)p(hobus) to him Helen & Paris
> exit Panda(r)us, exeunt omnes.

This seems to be based on *Troilus and Criseyde* Bk. II, 1394 ff.
and Bk. III in which the lovers achieve their first stolen meetings.
Chaucer's Pandarus gets Deiphebus (Troilus's favourite brother) to
invite Criseyde to his house and Troilus too on the excuse that she
needs a champion against her enemies (II. 1430–58). Next day
Criseyde comes with Antigone and Tarbe. Pandarus, telling
Criseyde that Troilus is sick, persuades her to enter his bedroom,
while Helen and Deiphebus are talking in the garden. Criseyde
lets Troilus know that she loves him, but no more is done that day

for Helen and Deiphobus come upstairs (III. 205). Soon afterwards Pandarus invites Criseyde to supper, and when it begins to
rain asks her to stay the night, then introduces Troilus into the
house and persuades Criseyde to receive him (III. 512 ff.). They
make love while Pandarus sits with his candle in the chimney. He
later brings them to bed again (III. 1667–94).

In the play apparently Troilus is brought by Pandarus at night
to meet Criseyde. She enters as if from her room with her waiting
maid and page (Mr. Jones his boy). (Shakespeare gives her a
servant, Alexander (*TC* I. 2).) The lovers converse with Pandarus and then go off, presumably to bed. Pandarus soliloquizes.
Deiphobus enters (perhaps because it is his house), then goes out
and returns with Helen and Paris. There are thus two pairs of
lovers in the house, and no doubt Helen and Paris discuss their own
affairs and the love of Troilus and Cressida. This scene is un-
doubtedly a climax of the play.

Scene F

E(n)ter Priam, Hect(o)r, Deiphobus, Paris
H(elen?) Cassandra to them *deleted* exit
De(iphob)us & Enter (w^th ?) Ulisses and

In Shakespeare Troilus, on the night when he first sleeps with
Cressida, gets Pandarus to ask Paris 'that, if the King call for him
at supper, you will make his excuse'. This leads to questions from
Paris and Helen. Perhaps Scene F begins with references to
Troilus's absence. The presence of Cassandra implies serious dis-
cussion, probably about Antenor's capture, the possibility of an
exchange, and perhaps about Helen's position. In Lydgate and
Caxton Paris several times refuses to let her go.

The coming of Ulysses with others—perhaps Diomed and even
Calchas (the traitor-priest, Cressida's father)—suggests the Greek
embassy to ask for a truce in Lydgate (*TB*. III. 3664–3754) and
Caxton (601–602). No doubt the exchange of Cressida is agreed
here as in Chaucer (IV. 57–217).

'This trewes duryng the Kynge Thoas was deliveryd in the
stede of Anthenor that they held prisoner whom they sente to

the Trojans . . . [Calcas] prayd to Kynge Agamenon and to
the other prynces that they wolde requyre the Kynge Pryant to
send Breseyda to hym. [Many Trojans disliked the idea.]
Alleway at the petycion of the Grekes the Kynge Pryant sente
Breseyda to her fader' (C. 601–602).

Perhaps Hector as in Chaucer (IV. 176–96) speaks against returning Cressida because she 'is no prisoner', and 'We usen here no
wommen for to selle'; and Cassandra foretells what Chaucer
recalls, that Antenor 'was after traitour to the toun/Of Troye.
Alas, they quitte him out too rathe' (IV. 203–204).

What happened in the five or six missing scenes which should
follow is even more doubtful. We should expect to see the parting between Troilus and Cressida (cf. Chaucer IV, 1123–1701),
and the exchange (Chaucer V. 1 ff.). The seduction of Cressida
by Diomed must also have been shown; possibly also her dismissal, though this may have been omitted since the story was
well known.

The Troilus-Cressida material must have been interspersed with
epic scenes. In one of them Ajax probably fought Hector.
Unfortunately the Plot affords no clue to when Achilles first
refused to fight, though presumably he *did* refuse since he does not
appear until Scene J. The absence of the Greeks' champion must
have been explained early in the play. Achilles' reluctance may
have been attributed to malcontent egoism, as in Shakespeare,
where Ulysses (I. 3. 142–210) describes him and Patroclus as
mocking the cautious policy of their elders. Since however
Polyxena appears in Scenes L and M it is possible that his with-
drawal was caused, as in the medieval sources, by love for her and
consequent desire for peace, and not, as in Homer, by his quarrel
with Agamemnon (who appears in the Plot, if at all, only in the
last scene) over Briseis. In Lydgate and Caxton Achilles' passion
for Polyxena was aroused when he first saw her during a truce
on the anniversary of Hector's death; but it may have been
anticipated. The play changes the order of events in other
ways; the death of Patroclus is put later than in the medieval
authorities.

Scene G

E(nter?)

D(e?)

This scene probably ran to two lines, and may have included an 'Alarum'. If Deiphobus was present, Troilus or Hector may have been there too. If 'D' is Diomed the dismissal of Cressida might be shown or referred to here.

Scene H

Alarum Enter

Diomede, menalay

& beat Hector in

Lydgate and Caxton (*TB*. III. 4449–82; *C*. 606–607) tell how, after the exchange-truce ended, Achilles (not as yet sulking) slew many noble men.

'Hector (writes Caxton) was this day sore hurte in the visage, and bledde grete plente of blood, and wyste not who had doon yt. And therfore the Trojans reculed unto the walles. And whan Hector behelde and sawe upon the wallis the quene Hecuba hys moder and his susters he had grete shame.'

Hector rallied, tumbled Achilles under his horse, and said to him: 'Achilles, Achilles, thou contendest to approche to me. Knowe that thou approchest thy deth.' They were separated by Troilus.

Since Achilles is not named and the fight does not continue after Hector is forced into the town (and also in view of the directions for Scene J) it seems likely that Achilles does not take part in this battle. The spectators on the walls may have been mentioned in the first line. There may be a reminiscence of this incident in Shakespeare at I. ii. where we are told that Queen Hecuba and Helen have gone 'up to the eastern tower' to watch the battle, and that Hector is enraged and ashamed because yesterday Ajax struck him down.

Scene I
> Alarum Enter Hector and Antenor *struck out,* Priam Mr.
> Jones *struck out* Antenor.

For the second time the writer of the Plot had difficulty with
Priam and Antenor. Perhaps Mr. Jones played both parts. Note
that in Scene D Priam is not on the walls when Antenor is captured.
It is hard to say what this scene included, but perhaps Antenor,
who had recently been in the Greek camp spoke about the
present battle, Diomed's treatment of Cressida and Achilles'
reluctance to accept Hector's challenge. This would lead on
naturally to the next scene.

Scene J
> Alarum Enter Diomede to Achil(lis Tent) to them Menalay,
> to them Ulisses to them Achillis in his Tent to them
> Aiax wth Patroclus on his back . exeunt

This departs from the chief authorities, who make Patroclus's
corpse the centre of a great battle. In Homer Hector is taking
Achilles's armour from the body when Ajax drives him off and
protects the dead man with his shield, exhorting the Greeks

> to abide,
> And no man fly the corse a foot, nor break their ranks in pride

Ajax also gets Menelaus to send Antilochus 'To tell Achilles
that his friend, most dear to him, is dead'. The Greeks are able
to carry off the body only when Achilles, roused from his
lethargy and armed by Minerva, enters the combat. Then they
'hearsed it, bearing it to fleet'. Lydgate (III. 892–6) and Caxton
(580–81) say less of this battle and make King Meryon carry off
the body.

With memories of Falstaff taking Hotspur's body on his back
to win undeserved honour (1H4. V. iv. 4. 129) we could easily see
the Admiral's Ajax as a buffoon like Shakespeare's; but Homer's
narrative makes it more probable that Ajax, though maybe coarse
and boastful, is here the gallant saviour of Patroclus' body, and
that his account of the mêlée makes Achilles return to war. This

heroic climax is followed by a pathetic and moral climax in Scene K.

Scene K

>   Enter Cressida, wth Beggars, pigg
>   Stephen, mr. Jones his boy. & mutes
>   to them Troylus, (& Deipho) bus & proctor
>   exeunt.

The source is clearly Henryson's *Testament of Cresseid* (ascribed to Chaucer in sixteenth-century editions of the latter). The scene is obviously that in which Cressida, now a leper, was with the other beggars (speaking parts played by Pigg, Stephen and 'Mr. Jones's boy' (her page in Scene E)) when Troilus and his men,

> With greit tryumphe and Laude victorious
> Againe to Troy richt Royallie thay raid
> The way quhair Cresseid with the Liper baid.[1]

The Lepers cried for alms, and Troilus, full of pity, came near the spot

> Quhair Cresseid sat, not wotting quhat scho was. . . .
> Than upon him ane blenk it come into his thocht,
> The he sumtime hir face befoir had sene,
> Bot scho was in sic plye he knew hir nocht,
> Yit than hir luik into his mynd it brocht
> The sweit visage and amorous blenking
> Of fair Cresseid sumtyme his awin darling.

Strangely moved, he took a girdle, a purse of gold, and many jewels, and dropped them into Cresseid's skirt, then rode away, 'and not ane word he spak,/Pensive in hart'.

Greg suggested that the scene in the play was invented to show an earlier phase in Cressida's life when (before she left Troy) she presumably gave alms to the beggars she was later to join. It is however most unlikely that the Admiral's dramatists would have room for or would desire to insert a scene which would exist

---

[1] Cited here from the edition by Bruce Dickins, 1925.

simply for its ironic effect. What could be more fitting at this stage in the drama when Achilles is returning to battle than Henryson's conclusion to the Troilus-Cressida relationship? Force is added to this argument by the presence of the 'proctor'. In Henryson the leper-folk gather round Cressida 'To se the equall distributioun/Of the Almous'. Now a proctor was an official who collected alms on behalf of lepers and others forbidden to beg for themselves. His presence in the play was probably suggested by Henryson's phrase. The scene would end with Cressida's bitter remorse on realizing her benefactor's identity ('O fals Cresseid, and trew Knicht Troylus').

Scene L

> Ente(r) Priam. Hector, Paris Hellena
> Cassan(d)ra Polixina to the(m) Antenor

This scene, bringing together Polyxena and the ill-boding Cassandra as well as Paris and Helen, Hector and their father, may well have included discussion of Achilles' desire for Polyxena and the possibility of peace. Antenor may enter to announce that Achilles is determined to avenge Patroclus. This may lead to discussion of Hector's challenge and his family's fears on his behalf. Andromache, whose dream in Lydgate (III. 4897–5140) makes Priam forbid his son to go out that day, is absent. But in Lydgate Hecuba, Helen, Cassandra and Polyxena also beg Hector to stay at home. He is furious, and when his half-brother Margariton is killed he rushes into the fray. Soon afterwards he is slain by Achilles.

Scene M

> Alarum   Enter D(io)med. & Troylus. to the(m)
>   Achillis. (t)o them Hector & Deipho(bus)
>   to them on the walls Priam Paris
> a re(treat) Hellen Polixina & Cassan(dra) to the(m)
>   ulisses Aiax Menalay & A(g)a
>   Priam & they on the wall desce(nd) to th(em)

The last extant directions, like the first, are for an important scene which brings together the main characters on both sides in the war. The meeting of Diomed and Troilus to an 'Alarum' must relate to one of several combats between them in Lydgate and Caxton. Achilles' coming probably forces Troilus to withdraw. Achilles is then attacked by Hector who is killed in sight of most of his family on the walls. As Tatlock suggested, the presence of Deiphobus 'seems to be a reminiscence from the Iliad XX, 227 ff. where just before Hector's death Athene stands by him in the form of Deiphobus'. Athene does it to cause Hector's death. Since there are apparently no deities in the play, Deiphobus must appear in his own person. Maybe he is kept occupied by Diomed or watches the duel. No Homeric chase round the walls is indicated, and the combats cease with the sounding of a 'retreat'. The Greek leaders enter and the royal Trojans come down to them presumably for formal negotiations. Maybe the Trojans plead for Hector's body.

Perhaps the play went on to show the slaying of Troilus by Achilles and his myrmidons (as in Lydgate IV, 2622-79 and Caxton p. 639), and the ceremonial mourning for Hector, but I incline to believe that it ended with Scene M.

Our findings about the Henslowe *Troilus and Cressida* may be summarized thus: It was a longish piece with many changes of scene but set mainly within or just outside the walls of Troy. Only one of the scenes indicated shows the Greek camp. Probably in the main the play took the Trojan point of view. It interwove two aspects of the war, the heroic and the erotic. In the heroic scenes Hector was the central Trojan figure, Ajax the chief Greek, until after the death of Patroclus in Scene J. Diomed was also brought to the fore, no doubt because of his rivalry with Troilus, and he was made the principal captor of Antenor. Antenor's part was magnified because, according to Lydgate and Caxton, he was Priam's first ambassador to the Greeks after Hesione's capture, his own capture and exchange were the cause of Cressida's removal from Troy, and later he was the chief negotiator for peace (C. 655). He betrayed Troy by obtaining the Palladium (C. 661-4) and by advising Priam to have the great horse taken into the city (C. 665-6).

Deiphobus too makes many appearances, as companion to Hector and Troilus. Neither Hecuba nor Andromache appears in the fragmentary Plot; Agamemnon only (if at all) in the last surviving scene. No doubt other highlights of the Troilus-Cressida story than those now indicated were shown. The appearance of Paris and Helen in at least four scenes was probably to allow the fatal effect of passionate love to be discussed in both the political and the Troilus-Cressida scenes.

The play was loosely episodic in structure but was planned with some thought for balance between characters, continuity in theme, dramatic variety, and contrast in tone. On the whole it followed the order of events in Lydgate and Caxton, but the death of Patroclus was put later (as in Homer) and Achilles' passion for Polyxena may have been put earlier. The Plot helps to counter the arguments of those critics who assert that Shakespeare followed only one source in writing each of his plays, since here we have two playwrights writing rapidly but consulting four or five authorities at least.

About the tone of the lost play little can be said with complete assurance. It contains no Thersites and no obvious clown. But Pandarus would probably be treated in traditional fashion as a comic figure and Ajax may or may not have been humorously represented.. The end of Cressida must however have been poignant and moral, certainly not satiric. What we know of Dekker suggests that he would not mock at heroism or love. His epic scenes would have a simplified Marlovian loftiness like the speeches of Fortune and Fortunatus in *Old Fortunatus* (I. 1), and Cressida on her last appearance might well utter sentimental truisms like those of Bellafront in *The Honest Whore, Pt. II*. In *Histriomastix* (probably revised by Marston in 1599) a player mockingly recites lines allegedly from a play:

> Come Cressida, my Cresset light,
> Thy face doth shine by day and night;
> Behold, behold, thy garter blue
> Thy knight his valiant elbow wears,
> That when he shakes his furious Spear

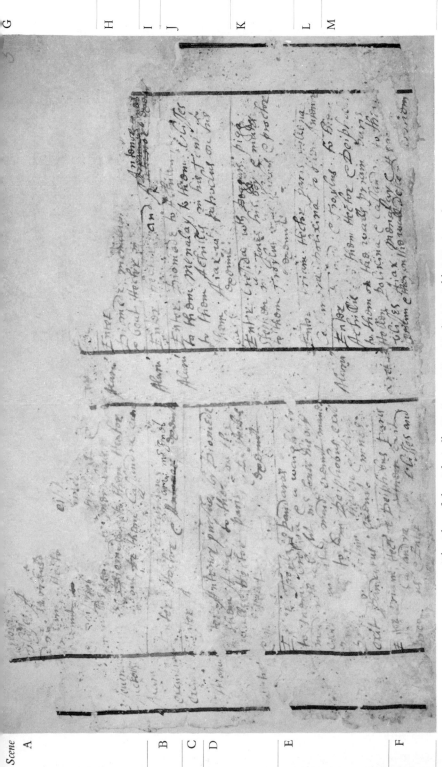

The Plot of the Admiral's *Troilus and Cressida* (B.M. Add. MS. 10449)

Photo: *British Museum*

STRATFORD FESTIVAL THEATRE, ONTARIO: 1. View of the Amphitheatre (2258 seats)

(*Photo: Peter Smith*)

The foe in shivering fearful sort
May lay him down in death to snort, &c. (ii. 269 ff.).

The hit was possibly at Dekker and Chettle's recent piece. If so the lost *Troilus and Cressida* was marked by high passion and rhetoric. 'Lame stuff indeed; the like was never heard', Marston makes one of the audience comment: but the parody may have been unjust.

Shakespeare's *Troilus and Cressida* has many similarities. It also is a 'multi-source' play, drawing on Caxton and (probably) Lydgate, Homer, Chaucer, and perhaps Ovid, but not directly on Henryson, though knowledge of Cressida's fate is implied. The story interweaves love and war, and the bedding of Troilus and Cressida occurs at the middle of the play. The death of Patroclus is set later than in the sources, and is not shown on the stage. Nestor's 'Go bear Patroclus' body to Achilles' is followed at once by Ulysses' assertion that 'Patroclus' wounds have roused his drowsy blood' (V. v. 17, 32). Shakespeare does not show Achilles' grief at receiving his friend's body, perhaps to avoid arousing our sympathy for either.

There are more conference scenes in Shakespeare, whose Trojans not only parley with the Greeks (as in the Admiral's Plot A, F and M), but also debate among themselves the continuance and conduct of the war (II. ii.) as do the Greeks themselves (I. iii, II. iii). Like Dekker and Chettle (in J) Shakespeare shows Achilles' comrades trying to persuade him to join the battle—not once however, but twice (II. iii; III. iii).

Shakespeare also introduces the Polyxena motif, unexpectedly, without proper preparation, for his Achilles, at first just an 'angry young man', is suddenly declared by Ulysses in III, iii. 19-209 to be 'in love/With one of Priam's daughters . . . And better would it fit Achilles much/To throw down Hector than Polyxena'. Also he has been in communication with Hecuba. This scene probably corresponds to Scene J in the Plot. The others which may be closest in the two plays are Scenes A and E. But there are other resemblances, in the balancing of characters (e.g. Helen and Paris against Troilus and Cressida (Scene E)) and in making a fight between Diomed and Troilus (Scene M) shortly

precede a meeting of Hector and Achilles (Scene M, cf. *T & C* V.
6). Shakespeare also introduces the Greek leaders rejoicing at
news of Hector's death (V. 8) so that his V. 6–8 seem to corre-
spond to much of Scene M. But Shakespeare does not have
Hector's death seen from the walls, or pass on to a meeting
between Trojan and Greek nobles; for his play is not a tragedy but
a satiric 'history' in which he scourges both sides for their false
notions of honour, traces in detail Troilus's rude awakening from
his calf-love, and, having effectively shown the hollowness of
epic and romance, ends suddenly, with Hector dead and Troilus
raging for revenge.

It has been argued that in Thersites or Ajax Shakespeare was
satirizing Dekker. There is no good evidence for either view.
But after comparing the two *Troilus and Cressida* plays it is difficult
to avoid the conclusion that Shakespeare's piece owed something
both positively and negatively to Dekker and Chettle's potboiler,
which anticipated not only the general lay-out of his material but
also several of his most important scenes. What Shakespeare did
was to rehandle his predecessors' double theme with an unroman-
tic, unsentimental and unheroic bias. Doubtless he was influenced
by the satiric spirit of the new century, and maybe by personal
considerations as well, but surely one element in his imaginative
approach to the Troy story was a desire to do better than Dekker
and Chettle, and to show how different the same material could
be made to seem if treated with 'modern' realism. So Achilles
becomes a treacherous wolf and Ajax a confusion of humours,
Cressida a wanton who does not suffer or repent, and Troilus a
boy in the throes of a delusive passion. Not content with having
Pandarus as a humorous observer Shakespeare follows Jonson and
the recent satiric vogue by introducing Thersites (from a hint in
Homer), and developing him into a cynical commentator, a
scurrilous mocker at good and evil alike.

Behind them all glow faintly the lost ideals of order in the state
and in individual life; but their world has turned its back on these,
and we may almost excuse the cynic for crying out in pleased disgust: 'Wars and lechery! nothing else holds fashion.'

IV

A Moniment Without a Tombe: The Stratford Shakespearian Festival Theatre, Ontario

MICHAEL J. SIDNELL

The more I see of these performances . . . the more I am convinced that their method of presenting a play is not only the
right method for that particular sort of play but that any play
performed on a platform amidst the audience gets closer home
to its hearers than when it is presented as a picture framed by a
proscenium. . . . All the old-fashioned tale of adventure plays,
with their frequent changes of scene, and all the new problem
plays, with their intense intimacies, should be done in this way.[1]
(George Bernard Shaw.)

Like literary criticism, the production of Shakespeare's plays
has tended at certain moments more to an awareness of the work
in its historical setting and, at others, more to an acknowledge-
ment of an evolutionary process through which our view of the
work has been substantially modified by later, particularly contemporary, conventions. The literary critic who finds his position
too precarious may correct his equilibrium covertly and by
degrees. In the theatre, to redress shortsightedness, error or out-
worn fashion involves much persuasion, money and the fortitude
to meet the public gaze, for critical views are architecturally
embodied and critical battles fought not only by the books but by
bricks, steel and concrete.

At Stratford, Ontario, the first critical stance was devised in
concrete, timber and canvas: the tent, determined by financial
and economic considerations, held architectural implications

---

[1] Shaw, G. B. Referring to William Poel's production of *Dr. Faustus* on a
stage after the model of the Fortune playhouse at St. George's Hall in 'The
Spacious Times', *The Saturday Review* (London, 11 July 1896). Reprinted in
Our Theatres in the Nineties (London, 1932), ii. 184.

which the designers and architects were later, and with genius, to seize upon.

In July 1952 at the first consultation with the visionary company of founders (the sociology of the foundation is worthy of study in itself) Sir Tyrone Guthrie suggested his kind of compromise for a modern Shakespearian theatre between the 'most conscientious possible reproduction of the original, the fruit of archaeological research' and 'the best available contemporary technique . . . as little beholden as possible to the past'.[1] At this time omitting theoretical and practical considerations, says Guthrie, 'I was merely suggesting that the best practical results would be gotten from a stage which closely conformed to what is known of the stage for which Shakespeare wrote and by relating the audience to that stage in a manner which approximated to the Elizabethan manner.'[2] And when Tanya Moseiwitsch had been appointed designer she and Guthrie agreed, he says, 'that while conforming to the conventions of the Elizabethan theatre in practicalities, [the stage] should not present a pseudo-Elizabethan appearance. We were determined to eschew Ye Olde'.[3]

Architecturally, the Stratford Theatre is in its third phase: the original tent created over a concrete amphitheatre was in use from the opening in 1953 until the end of the 1956 season: the permanent theatre building was erected over the same base and a very slightly modified stage for the 1957 season: the remodelled stage was first used in the 1962 season. (See plates facing pages 39, 54 and 55.)

That the concrete amphitheatre takes advantage of a natural declivity on the site makes for a satisfying external architecture and, more important, it is one of those features more Greek in inspiration than Elizabethan which, from the moment one passes into the auditorium, give a sense of a relationship with the stage for which 'intimacy' the usual term, seems insufficient: there is in this relationship intensity and expectancy, tautness rather than relaxation, arising from the pronounced centripetal tendency of the design. The centric stage, the absence of a pit, the steeply

[1] Adumbrated long before in his *Theatre Prospect* (London, 1932), p. 48.

[2] *A Life in the Theatre* (London, 1960), p. 284.

[3] Ibid., p. 286.

banked seats and large auditorium sector are basic factors making
for the intensity of 'ritual'—a term commonly used to describe
Stratford productions and one to which I shall recur.

In designing the permanent theatre, the architects took their
principal inspiration from the tent it was to replace. The circular
building, 200 feet in diameter, is capped by a conical roof. Inside,
the wide outer ring of the blue fluted ceiling repeats the cone, and
an acoustic disc 32 feet in diameter suspended immediately above
the stage flattens the conical form. The orchestra loft is placed
immediately behind the main apron and 22 feet above it: as close
as it can be to the acoustical (and geometrical) centre of the building. In the permanent building, apart from backstage facilities
and a small rehearsal theatre, a balcony was added to give a total
of 2,258 seats, none more than 65 feet from the stage, and the
audience sector was reduced to an arc of 220^0. The exterior and
interior of the building suggest a stylization of a circus pavilion,
and the resulting tension between plastic and geometrical forms is
characteristic of the theatre, the stage and its use at Stratford.

The addition of two window balconies above the side entrance
was the only significant alteration made to the stage when the
permanent theatre was erected. Before the remodelling of 1961–2,
there were six entrances cut into the façade: a main entrance
giving into the 'inner-stage' below the gallery balcony, an
entrance giving on to the gallery balcony immediately above,
and side entrances from which the actor would descend five
steps from a small platform to pass under the gallery or ascend
six steps to the gallery balcony; above each side entrance was a
window balcony. Projecting from the façade, the low gallery
was supported by a bosket of nine pillars. The shape of the
gallery platform in relation to the arc of the auditorium, the cone
of the roof and the radial half of the façade, was and remains a
distinctive feature of the theatre: this platform may be seen as a
square with one of the angles salient and the opposite angle set
into the façade. The gallery pillars stood on an 'island' riser
from which the actors would descend to the main apron stage.
The apron was stepped, on five sides, into an encircling 'gutter'.

In the autumn of 1961, this stage was redesigned by Tanya

Moseiwitsch in association with the present production designer
Brian Jackson. 'The decision to alter the stage,' goes the official
comment, 'came from a need to correct technical difficulties that
had arisen over nine years.'[1] At the theatre I was told[2] that the
main objectives of the remodelling were: a desire to make the
stage more 'masculine'; a need for stronger entrances; a firmer
suggestion of more than one house or location in the façade.
Before the alterations there had been two main kinds of adverse
criticism of the Stratford stage: objections to weak entrances and
objections to the very architectural conception. The former were
met by the remodelling. The original side entrances with the
windows and balconies above them were eliminated and in their
stead two soaring Craigian panels were hinged to provide entrances when required. Two new side entrances were cut farther
out in the façade giving on to larger platforms from which the
actor descends four steps to the main apron stage (no longer
having to pass beneath the gallery). The clump of nine slender
gallery supports was replaced by five thicker and taller pillars
raising the gallery eight inches. The single 'brow' which had
contained and unified the entrances from window to window
was replaced by a series of five canopies (cabbalists will recognize
in the pentarsic design a more tragic theatre). The remodelling
effectively answers such criticisms of the old stage as this:

> Its six major entrances, excluding the long rushes down the
> aisles, afford no actor a dominant approach to the central
> acting area. If he comes on either left or right upstage, the
> impact of his appearance is lost or dissipated for the right or
> left segments of the audience. If he comes on dead centre and
> upstage, the pillars supporting the upper levels force him to
> weave his way forward, making that sudden movement of
> confrontation, which is the heart and essence of drama, impos-
> sible. The central entrance on the upper level leaves the actor
> in a void which serves very well to suggest a balcony and little

[1] 'The Shakespearian Festival', p. 3, an undated, anonymous mimeographed
pamphlet of four pages distributed from the theatre in 1962.

[2] I am indebted to many members of the Production Staff and Company,
past and present, for information and observations on every aspect of the
theatre.

more. This leaves the burrowed entrances under the audience, which face the stage and therefore have their major impact as exits, since the actor can face the major part of the audience only when he is going off.[1]

The side entrances are now dominant approaches. The centre entrance has become stronger with the reduced number of gallery pillars, though the pillar supporting the salient angle of the gallery-platform remains. This pillar, being dead centre of the entrance, deflects the actor using it from his path or divides two or more actors. If a cantilever were used, the pillar could be eliminated with the consequence of a stronger upstage entrance and more open 'inner stage'. But the space beneath the gallery has not been used as an inner stage and it has been avoided for important locations. Fussy movement within and around the enclosure of the pillars is appropriate for Sir Toby and his companions spying on Malvolio but not for the murder of Desdemona (whose bed was placed on the main apron). Again, the principal advantage of the space beneath the gallery is perhaps that the entrances and exits are not 'strong'. Instead of being eclipsed by the wings or propelled through them, the actor is received by and emerges from more than a hole in the wall. He goes inside something, is *by degrees* lost to sight and our sense of an imagined action off-stage is sustained. Though the actors play very little beneath the gallery, the space is frequently used to suggest an interior structure which the audience imagines as extending over the main stage.

That the actors using the main side entrances no longer have to pass beneath the gallery reduces the importance of the pillar enclosure. This new feature, together with the more expansive façade, bigger platform areas and the elimination of the balconies give more emphasis to the Greek and correspondingly less to the Elizabethan aspects of the stage. The old seems rather complicated and involved in contrast with the new stage when one sees the models side by side.

[1] Ferry, A., 'The Tyranny of the Stratford Stage', *The Canadian Forum* (August 1960), pp. 106–8.

Serious considerations of the Stratford stage have been rather obscured by expressions of patriotic pride, exhortations to support, souvenir publications, open-stage polemics and encomia, but some there have been, and not all favourable. Richard Leacroft, in an article which contains some questionable theory of dramatic presentation, finds that:

It is difficult to introduce scenic elements on to this form of projecting stage . . . only such items and levels as do not block audience sight-lines being possible; so that in these theatres the producer must accept the limitations of preconceived architectural forms, which inevitably impose limitations on the variations in production movement that may be made either from or to pre-selected entry ways, or in a change of level. The projection forward of the Stratford stage-balcony cuts off the sight lines to the stairs, so that it is possible for an actor using these to be cut off from the sight of a large section of the audience, with consequent loss of dramatic tension.[1]

As to the 'scenic elements', Mr. Leacroft's objections would be dismissed by the Stratford producers and many others for well-known reasons. The lavishly executed properties and costumes at Stratford would satisfy all but the most gluttonous consumer of 'scenic elements'. What he says about the sight lines is true, though the bold corollary is surely false. One invariably knows what the actor is doing and where he is going. That he is momentarily (or, as one of a crowd, more than that) out of sight may have nothing to do with 'dramatic tension' and may be used to heighten it. For the actor to be visible all the time he is on stage or (as, George F. Reynolds has recently suggested)[2] for the actor to be invisible when he is 'off' stage are conventions which have

[1] 'Actor and Audience Part Two: I' *Journal of the Royal Institute of British Architects* Vol. 70, No. 4 (London, April 1963), p. 151. In this article Mr. Leacroft makes no mention of the new stage and is clearly speaking of the stage as it was before the 1962 season. The changes have no material bearing on the passage quoted, though Mr. Leacroft's strictures elsewhere could, in view of the date of publication, be misleading.

[2] 'Two Conventions of the Open Stage (as illustrated in *King Lear*)' *Philological Quarterly*, xli (Chapel Hill, N. Carolina, 1962), pp. 82–95.

no simple connection with 'dramatic tension'. I will not pursue the point to distinguish between an optimum and a maximum of 'dramatic tension' but merely observe that Agatha Christie probably yields more of it per play than Shakespeare. But Leacroft's most important objection is one that is shared by others and has much relevance to Shakespearian and other theatres at the present time. The producer at Stratford must indeed accept 'preconceived architectural forms'. It seems to me the greatest triumph of Stratford that it has evolved from experiment to style at a time when 'flexibility' and 'experimental' have such rallying power as catchwords in the theatre. There is at Stratford a certain simple acceptance of an architectural fact: the theatre has become an instrument for the production of Shakespeare's plays by contrast with those theatres where the plays have been used as though they were a vivisector's specimens to be mutilated in the interests of the science of the theatre. For eleven years, Shakespeare has been performed at Stratford not always to the critical applause of the judicious but with a consistency of style probably unequalled anywhere else. As a sustained and successful attempt to establish modern conventions for the performance of Shakespeare to a wide public, Stratford continues to be a stable centre amidst the flux of experiment.

In recent years a number of memorials to technological ingenuity have been erected in the guise of theatres. They have been devised ostensibly for the purpose of presenting Sophocles and Shakespeare, Ibsen and Ionesco, Ben Jonson and Brecht in the kind of setting envisaged by the playwrights for their plays. The efforts made by Shaw and Ibsen in many of their best, and especially later, plays to escape from the convention of the fourth wall, go unnoticed by those who fear that lacking a proscenium arch and facilities for flying scenery we would cut ourselves off from an important part of our dramatic tradition. One might observe that a good play is more 'adaptable' and 'flexible' than building materials can ever be: or even with Walter Kerr (and the Shaw of the epigraph) 'that however closely Shakespeare's playhouse was related to the particular spirit of a particular time, it also embraced principles that were in some way universal, that it belonged—as our theatre buildings do not quite belong—to some sort of main-stream'.[1]

There is an aspect of Shakespearian production which tends nowadays to be treated as a contaminated area: its influence on contemporary playwrights. The admonitions of Yeats, Eliot and others on the dangers of imitating Shakespearian verse and drama-tic form have had a lasting influence in historical and critical accounts of nineteenth- and twentieth-century drama.

As an alternative to the view that nineteenth-century poets failed as dramatists through the lack of an adequate theatrical technique, Eliot offered his conviction that Shakespearian blank verse, having 'lost the flexibility which blank verse must have if it is to give the effect of conversation', had been a kind of gravita-tional force pulling poet-dramatists to their destruction. But might we not re-diagnose the failure, with its verbal and technical symptoms as arising from the dilemma of the playwright (prose-writer and poet, then and now) in his search for viable conven-tions? On the one hand he is presented with the conventions embodied in the plays of his greatest predecessors but for which his theatre offers few physical counterparts; on the other, equally unsatisfactorily, he has the conventions current in the theatre but too tenuously connected with the core of our dramatic tradition. Eliot chose the Scribean theatre's 'laws' of 'dramatic relevance' to order his verse; Yeats first attempted to make his own theatre and then withdrew his plays from the public stage altogether. Both have been seminal playwrights and theorists from whom we may yet trace a new harmony in the theatre of the individual talent with tradition. Perhaps Ibsen, had he remained in the theatre, could have spanned the theatrical gulf between Shakespeare and Scribe, but the playwright's dilemma remains and it is made the more acute by the anarchy of adaptable theatres.

Stratford issues a new invitation to the playwright and his audience to reassemble the fragments of a tradition. The invita-tion is articulated by the architectural attributes of the theatre and in its announced and effected policy of producing plays other than

[1] Kerr, Walter, 'The Theatre Breaks Out of Belasco's Box', *Horizon* (New York, July 1959), pp. 41–8.

Shakespeare's, including modern and new works. So far three non-Shakespearian productions have been staged: *Oedipus Rex* in Yeats's version, *Cyrano de Bergerac,* and *The Canvas Barricade* by a contemporary Canadian playwright, Donald Jack. *Cyrano* and *Oedipus* were both notably successful and repeated in a second season. If the hoped-for new dramatists successfully exploit the Stratford theatre they will no doubt have much to do with the shaping of the attitudes of a new generation not only to its contemporary drama but to our dramatic tradition and to the plays of Shakespeare in particular: the really telling confirmation of the permanence of Shakespeare's art will come in successive generations not solely from critics, actors, scholars, directors and architects but also from playwrights neither imitating nor fearful of imitation but at ease with a tradition.

Antony Ferry, in some incisive remarks, has suggested that the Stratford theatre is so far from inviting as to be a fortress impregnable to the dramatists, and finally defeating Shakespeare and his best directors:

> The structure has stood in defiance of the best directors that money could import to the Festival. I am not sure that it does not emerge as the real victor. For what seems like an exciting conflict brings Shakespeare each time to his knees.[1]

Mr Ferry, writing of the 1960 season, anticipated in his criticisms some of the alterations which were made to the stage a year and a half later (particularly in the matter of entrances) but his central point is not answered by the re-modelling:

> The stage itself becomes the inflexible tyrant of each piece, and this is no more apparent than in *King John*. The emphasis on pomp and pageantry is an arbitrary requirement of the tiered platforms, as are the emptive entrances and excessive choreography that surrounds and muffles the force of the simplest spoken line.
> The myth of the Stratford stage is engendered by its aesthetic purity, which is immediate and visual but never functional.

[1] Op. cit., pp. 106–8.

The whole building is a perfectly designed microcosm that shows no flaws until it is put to work. . . . The difficulty in reaching the main acting area; the awkward entrance points, the masking of certain areas of the stage by the rigid central structure; and the fact that theatre-in-the-round means not one but three audiences to act for at once: these are the factors that force the company into arbitrary balletics.[1]

The kind of truth that lies in the comments can be discovered, in part, by letting the stage 'perform' without the adulteration of players and play. Walking around the auditorium in the empty theatre, the changing perspectives of the stage and its relationship with façade and auditorium offer the aesthetic satisfaction of a fine sculpture: visual harmony gives way to a succession of new harmonies. Only from the dead centre (where there are no seats) is the design dull and static in its symmetry. With a group motionless on it, the stage ceases to be sculptural and becomes architectural (for we are within the same space as the players) and as one moves round the auditorium a complex and satisfying choreographic illusion emerges. A director grouping and moving his players before the stationary audience is inescapably presented with choreographic problems and opportunities. Tyrone Guthrie and Michael Langham, Stratford's principal directors, have particularly stressed this aspect of production in practice and theory: with the 'choreography' goes 'ritual', the analogy of text and musical score, and (more outside the theatre than within) 'pageantry'. That the 'balletics' are not arbitrary in that they are partly given or imposed by the architecture is apparent: that Mr. Ferry does not care for them is equally so. And he is not alone. The heart of the objection seems to be to a theatre in which design is architectural. The actors are playing not to three audiences but to over 2,000 each with a somewhat different view of the action: to an arranged crowd rather than ranks of spectators. Nowadays, with Shakespeare squeezed into the tiniest box yet devised for dramatic performances, played as it were to a many-bodied cyclops, it has surely become clearer that, whatever kinds of

[1] Ibid., pp. 106–7.

dramatic expression be developing, the *theatre* is based above all upon a relationship between action, actors and audience in an architectural setting. Poel, with his reconstructed stage for *Measure for Measure*, escaped from the pictorial into the sculptural, with action and actors but not audience related to the 'permanent' structure—and such an escape is now commonly effected in theatres where no other is possible. Some three months before he was invited to advise on the Stratford project, Tyrone Guthrie in an address to the Shakespeare Stage Society dwelt on 'the next step':

> The Elizabethan theatre I have in mind would be large enough to pay its way, but small enough for the actors to be heard without speaking too loudly and slowing down their delivery. Since William Poel, producers have been grappling with this problem and have resorted to the enlarged forestage as at Stratford and the Old Vic. But this does not alter the fact that the stage is isolated at one end of a large hall. As a result, even with the enlarged forestage, the declamatory method is still necessary for the sake of audibility and consequently variety in tone and tempo in the verse-speaking is lost. In the Elizabethan theatre, with its stage projecting into the auditorium, the audience surrounded and hung over the cockpit when the play took place. Today there is confusion about the next step.[1]

Guthrie's next step was at Stratford. Ironically the tent theatre was unsatisfactory acoustically but more than a temporary resolution of architectural problems and controversies. The audience was at last under the same roof and inside the same space as the actors.

That Stratford is not an easy stage to work on is attested by the actors and demonstrated by some of them. Very subtle variations of voice, expression and movement are possible for an actor so intimately involved, spatially, with his audience. Likewise, crudities in diction and gesture, from which the Stratford company is not free, are accentuated: an awkward step (and many

---

[1] Quoted *William Poel and the Elizabethan Revival* (London, 1954), pp. 274–5.

steps are necessary on this stage), a hesitation or momentary loss of control in the voice, jar our senses grossly. Many actors fail to overcome the great difficulty of making themselves distinctly heard by the section of the audience behind or to the side without bellowing or declaiming at the auditors in front of them. Similarly some perform the difficult operation of presenting themselves to the various sections of the audience with the mechanical motion of a merry-go-round. Sometimes, too, the director moves his players so unsubtly as to make a see-saw of his efforts to balance the stage. Perhaps the most obvious defect in the acting on the Stratford stage is the tendency to approach high-flown rhetoric with excessive caution, even timidity. The lyrical romanticism of the 1963 *Cyrano de Bergerac* was delightfully managed but Rostand's formal and critical concern with rhetoric was suppressed. Again, the Trojan and Greek debates in *Troilus and Cressida* were presented in the same subtle and restrained way as the Cressida episodes: the intricacies of plot and character (of Cressida in particular) emerged in their full complexity but the rhetorical affirmations of Hector and Ulysses were obscured by an over-subtle characterization and tame delivery. This retreat from rhetoric seems in part determined by an excessive reaction against declamation and in part by the theatre itself. It would be too easy to split the ears of the audience at Stratford and, fearful of this, the actors tend to become more tame than discreet. What is clear is that the craft of playing at Stratford is extraordinarily complex and that it is not easily mastered even by experienced actors capable of good performances in other theatres and media. The stage affords opportunities for brilliant and subtle effects. They are achieved when the director and his associates can match the possibilities of the stage in rhythm, tempo and design and when the actors can meet the demands which, on this stage, the play and its directors must make of them.

The movements of the actors on a stage which is architecturally one with the auditorium must be arbitrary or choreographic. And it is primarily from the physical theatre, too, that the 'ritualism' of Stratford seems to proceed. The amphitheatre is strangely time-laden and familiar: the idea or remembrance of an Elizabethan or Greek theatre, the boxing-ring, bull-ring, bear-ring or circus may all, in some measure, be present. The audience is drawn to Stratford for what has become more truly a festival as the novelty has worn off and that affectation of condescension (no doubt of almost as ancient descent) to festivals which spreads apace, has had no appreciable effect. No modern audience can have 'that excitement and breathless anticipation which Shakespeare's audience felt when they crowded into the theatre in Shoreditch to see his new play about King John.[1] As a substitute it is offered too frequently the meretricious titillation of a zymotechnical production. Rarely has this kind of substitute been offered to Stratford audiences, although Guthrie's cowboy production of *The Taming of the Shrew* and Peter Coe's attempt to 'remove all the debris of the past' from *Macbeth* may be adduced as exceptions. It would be too much to expect that the Stratford, or any theatre could be for a modern audience 'a symbol of social order and of divine order—of the real ties between man and king, between heaven and earth'[2] but the architectural setting makes possible the intense re-enactment of 'a vision of man's central place in a cosmos of dignity and order'[3] in the production of Shakespeare there. Moreover, the theory of production has been neither to pretend that the audience can step back into the 'Elizabethan world picture' nor to attempt to apply Shakespeare to acosmic moderns. For this kind of production, neither 'pure' nor 'applied', of plays which at least seem familiar to almost all the audience (for even the sad ones who declare that for years Shakespeare was spoilt for them by a Holofernes, use that 'Shakespeare' with familiarity) 'ritual' seems a not inappropriate term. Between that representation of Shakespeare which has reduced the plays to a 'mythographic jumble' in an abyss of magic which obscures their mimetic basis and the naturalistic and illusionistic interpretations lately in fashion, Michael Langham has struck his balance:

[1] John Sisson, 'King John: A History Play for Elizabethans' in *Stratford Papers on Shakespeare*, 1961 (Toronto, 1960), pp. 1–19.

[2] George R. Kernodle, 'The Open Stage: Elizabethan or Existentialist?' in *Shakespeare Survey* 12 (Cambridge, 1959), p. 3.

[3] Ibid., p. 7.

The Philosophy of this Canadian Stratford is something like this: if you will work with the actors they will create for you the totality of life. This stage will not be some literal, fixed location but at any given moment will constitute the crucible in which the living elements of the play will interact. We do not ask our audiences to believe that what they are seeing is really taking place, as in real life. We ask them to indulge with us in a game of make-believe, but to retain sufficient objectivity to be conscious of the parallel between real life and this heightened, ritualistic performance of it.[1]

[1] Langham, M. 'Staging Shakespeare's Works' in *Stratford Papers on Shakespeare*, 1961 (Toronto 1962).

STRATFORD FESTIVAL THEATRE, ONTARIO: 2. Stage used from 1957 to 1961 (designed by Tanya Moiseiwitsch).

(Photo: Peter Smith)

STRATFORD FESTIVAL THEATRE, ONTARIO: 3. New stage, 1962 (designed by Tanya Moiseiwitsch in association with Brian Jackson).
Left to right: Brian Jackson, Tanya Moiseiwitsch, Michael Langham (Artistic Director).

(Photo: Peter Smith)

V

The Glass of Pandar's Praise:
The Word-Scenery, Mirror Passages, and Reported
Scenes in Shakespeare's 'Troilus and Cressida'

RUDOLF STAMM

THIS paper illustrates a kind of study in which the present writer
has become intensely interested as the result of a long series of
theatrical disappointments. In the period in which Alexander
Tairov's 'Entfesseltes Theater' flourished he saw a Hamlet, who,
acting his father's part in addition to his own, fell into a trance
and turned ventriloquist whenever the ghost spoke, a Hamlet
who climbed a specially constructed high tower in order to speak
the 'To be or not to be' soliloquy, a Lady Macbeth gliding along
the wall with trembling hands while she said:

That which hath made them drunk hath made me bold;

(II. ii. 1)

a Bassanio belonging to a ruffianly gang of brown-shirts which
hunted down an entirely noble Shylock. These and a great
number of similar experiences have convinced him that our
modern Shakespearian scholarship and criticism have failed to
define clearly and irrefutably the line where the modern theatrical
interpreter's sphere of freedom and originality begins and where
it ends, if a play is to be produced without serious loss and distortion. In order to work towards this definition it seems necessary
to take quite seriously the truism that the playwright's material
is different from that of the poet and the novelist. His means of
expression are not words alone, but words together with the
movements and gestures of living actors and with all the resources
of the stage. No true dramatist is without the desire to control

and manipulate not only the speeches of his characters, but his other means of expression as well. In modern plays we find ample stage directions describing the setting and the appearance, the movements, the gestures, the facial expression, perhaps even the intonation of the characters. In Shakespeare the scarcity and the casual treatment of such directions is surprising. This could lead a superficial observer to the belief that he was primarily the poet who took care of his characters' speeches and left the rest to his actor-friends and to the producers of later ages. The careful reader, however, discovers a great number of explicit and implicit references to place and time, sometimes developed into evocations of atmosphere, as well as to appearance, gestures and business in the speeches themselves. Shakespeare's word-scenery was naïvely misinterpreted by believers in the nineteenth-century picture-stage as the makeshift of a playwright whose misfortune it was to write for a stage with very limited scenic resources. It would be foolish to ignore the makeshift basis of his practice, but even more foolish to overlook how necessity became an important stimulus for his art. It pointed the way towards that entirely functional and organic use of place, time, and gesture which is a distinguishing mark of his mature plays.

Many scenes contain no indications of time or place; definitions of place and time, as well as atmospheric and symbolic settings, are only introduced when they are essential to the meaning. Similarly, innumerable details of appearance, gesture and business are taken for granted or barely hinted at. The playwright could rely on a solid acting tradition, which had evolved effective stage equivalents for the details of behaviour in the common situations of social life. In many rhetorical passages, too, there was no need for him to assume direct control of the mimetic interpretation, because his actor-friends knew how to respond in movement and gesture to the demands of the rhythm and the rhetorical figures.[1] There were other situations, however, where the playwright desired to control the gestic as well as the vocal expression of his meaning. He did this by introducing mirror passages and re-

[1] Cf. on this problem B. L. Joseph, *Elizabethan Acting* (Oxford University Press, 1951).

ported scenes. With the help of these devices he was not only able to influence the acting of particular passages; they enabled him to communicate to his actors and spectators glimpses of his complete creation, which consisted of speech and action; of emotions, impulses, and conflicts expressing themselves through the action of the speech organs as well as through their reflexes in the movements of the whole body of the actor. These glimpses can have and should have a stimulating and regulating influence on our imaginative experience of the whole play, not only of the situation or character directly concerned.

The study of the references to gestures and business, together with the place-time indications, makes visible the inner form of the play-in-performance. This inner form is not identical with any individual performance, historical or modern. It is part of the ideal existence of the play. Without its knowledge an adequate theatrical, or critical, interpretation of it would seem impossible in any period. Its investigation is by no means a new enterprise. Contributions to it have come from many different critics. Otto Ludwig, Bernard Shaw, Harley Granville-Barker and Richard Flatter are eminent among them. The incidental remarks of Ludwig, Shaw and many others, as well as the detailed books by Granville-Barker[1] and Flatter,[2] render a more methodical approach to our subject desirable. The lines it could follow are illustrated here by a study of the theatrical physiognomy of *Troilus and Cressida*.

We cannot undertake it without inquiring what the stage directions of the Q- and the F-text of the play contribute towards the definition of place, time, gesture and business. Those in Q 'are generally meagre',[3] those in F only a very little less so. They are mainly, but by no means consistently, concerned with entrances and exits and with stage sounds. Characteristically, they rarely add anything of importance to what is deducible from the speeches themselves.

[1] *Prefaces to Shakespeare* (London 1927-47).

[2] *Shakespeare's Producing Hand. A Study of His Marks of Expression to be Found in the First Folio* (London 1948).

[3] W. W. Greg, *The Shakespeare First Folio* (Oxford 1955), p. 341.

There is very little precise place and time definition in the play. The first line of the Prologue tells us:

> In Troy, there lies the scene.

The Prologue then offers a brief description of the earlier phases of the siege of 'Priam's six-gated city', and adds:

> that our play
> Leaps o'er the vaunt and firstlings of those broils,
> Beginning in the middle; starting thence away
> To what may be digested in a play.

Scene i. is 'placed' by Troilus' lines:

> Why should I war without the walls of Troy
> That find such cruel battle here within?
> (I. i, 2 f.)

It is their main function to express Troilus' inner situation; incidentally, however, they also 'place' the scene as a whole. Scene ii is vaguely characterized as a street scene in Troy by the coming and going of Trojan people. A topographical detail is added by Alexander's remark that Queen Hecuba and Helena are going

> Up to the eastern tower,
> Whose height commands as subject all the vale,
> To see the battle. (I. ii, 2 f.)

The hints concerning the elevated position from which Pandarus points out the returning war-lords to Cressida are left quite indefinite:

> Shall we stand up here and see them as they pass toward Ilium?
> (I. ii, 172)

> Here, here, here's an excellent place; here we may see most bravely. (I. ii, 175.)

These words from Pandarus are all we hear about it.

Instances of more definite 'placing' are rare in the play. Pandarus' 'Walk here i' th' orchard . . .' (III, ii, 16) and Ulysses' 'Achilles stands i' th' entrance of his tent' (III, iii, 38) should be mentioned here. The method of 'placing' a scene by a remark spoken in the preceding one is employed in V, i. when Ulysses tells Troilus:

Follow his torch; he goes to Calchas' tent; (V. i, 82).

Having heard it, we know where we are when Diomedes calls at the beginning of the next scene:

What, are you up here, ho? Speak. (V. ii, 1.)

Thus the place indications in our play are strictly, even severely, functional. The city of Troy and the Greek camp are the scene of the conflicts of love and war which are the theme of the play, but the poet withholds from them his power of giving atmospheric reality to a place. There are only a few picturesque touches. We have quoted the allusion to 'the eastern tower', and may add here the picture of the town called up by Ulysses when he reminds Hector of its doom:

> For yonder walls, that pertly front your town,
> Yond towers, whose wanton tops do buss the clouds,
> Must kiss their own feet. (IV. v, 219 f.)

Walls and towers, as seen by Ulysses, are alive with the pride of the Trojans. Similarly, the Greek tents are addressed as symbols of pride by Troilus at the end of the play. (V. x, 23 f.) Both these pieces of word-scenery create a certain sense of place, and contribute at the same time to our experience of the human passion which is the root of the War of Troy.

Shakespeare's allusions to time in *Troilus and Cressida* are functional, too. The fact that it is evening when the lovers are brought together by Pandarus is suggested by the situation itself and by remarks on the end of another day's fighting in the preceding scene. In the following scenes time indications are surprisingly scarce. At the beginning of Act IV the stage direction mentions torches to suggest a night scene. When Troilus is about to take leave of his mistress there are a few speeches to make us feel the early hour:

> *Tro.* Dear, trouble not yourself; the morn is cold.
>
> (IV. ii. 1)
>
> *Tro.* O Cressida! but that the busy day,
>   Wak'd by the lark, hath rous'd the ribald crows,
>   And dreaming night will hide our joys no longer,
>   I would not from thee.
> *Cres.*   Night hath been too brief.
>
> (IV. ii. 8 ff.)

At the opening of Scene iii the coming of the day and of the lovers' separation is succinctly mentioned:
> *Par.* It is great morning; and the hour prefix'd
>   For her delivery to this valiant Greek
>   Comes fast upon.   (IV. iii. 1 ff.)

The atmosphere and mood of the early morning count for comparatively little here. More important is the lovers' experience of time moving rapidly and rapaciously. It is communicated by the pressure of the events themselves and accentuated by the imagined bustling figures of 'injury of chance' and 'injurious time', coming alive in Troilus' complaint (IV. iv. 32 ff.).

Also the second great night scene of the play, in which Cressida breaks her vows under Troilus' eyes, is left with a minimum of atmosphere. We are prepared for the nocturnal meeting in the preceding scene by the good-night wishes of the heroes. Ulysses' reference to a torch in V. i. 82 is repeated in his first speech in the new scene:

> Stand where the torch may not discover us.
>
> (V. ii. 5)

The stars and the moon appear just once in Cressida's asseveration:

By all Diana's waiting women yond,
And by herself, I will not tell you whose.
(V. ii. 90 f.)

The one major use of word-scenery in the play appears near its close. Its atmospheric function is incidental to a symbolic one. It occurs in Achilles' speech immediately before the murder of Hector. There has not been anything in the series of battle scenes before the murder to make us conscious of the time of day, except Troilus' somewhat indefinite exclamation:

No, by the flame of yonder glorious heaven,
(V. vi. 23)

and Hector's declaration: 'Now is my day's work done' (V. viii. 3), which clearly points to an evening hour. In spite of this preparation there remains a certain incongruous purple patch quality about the grandiloquent speech in which Achilles acquaints Hector with his impending murder:

Look, Hector, how the sun begins to set;
How ugly night comes breathing at his heels;
Even with the vail and dark'ning of the sun,
To close the day up, Hector's life is done.
(V. viii. 5 ff.)

The image is completed after the murder:

The dragon wing of night o'erspreads the earth
And, stickler-like, the armies separates.
(V. viii. 17 f.)

The whole passage, evoking the image of the setting sun and the coming of night to accompany and render glorious the end of Hector, is appropriate to the nobility and importance of this hero, but it is hardly in keeping with the miserable circumstances of his death, and it sounds strange coming from the mouth of the trickster Achilles. It is a *tour de force* by which the playwright tried to save Hector's end from being too shocking an anticlimax.

Troilus and Cressida is definitely not an atmospheric play. Its author's attention was concentrated upon his figures, especially upon the influence of their characters on their actions and sufferings. Besides Troilus and Cressida themselves an unusual number of secondary figures are carefully drawn in sharp outline, and each of them is given his full life and individuality. Whereas wordscenery is scarce in the text, direct and indirect references to appearance, behaviour and business abound in it.

To begin with, we consider a number of mirror passages. The simplest kind is before us when a speaker accompanies a gesture of his own by its name. Agamemnon describes a ceremony of friendship, saying:

> Fair Lord Aeneas, let me touch your hand;
> To our pavilion shall I lead you, first.
> (I. iii. 304 f.)

Preparing the climax of the scene in which the lovers plight their troth, Pandarus arranges an impressive group with the words: 'Here I hold your hand; here my cousin's.' (III. ii. 193.) The following speech of Cressida's mirrors the action by which, in her anxious curiosity, she emphasizes her appeal to Pandarus: 'Good uncle, I beseech you, on my knees I beseech you, what's the matter?' (IV. ii. 87 f.) Pandarus' exclamation: 'Let me embrace too' (IV. iv. 14) names an action of his own, but tells us at the same time that Cressida embraced Troilus when she cried: 'O Troilus! Troilus!' (IV. iv. 12). And Troilus, too, throws light on the action of the farewell scene where he complains that 'injurious time'

> scants us with a single famish'd kiss,
> Distasted with the salt of broken tears.
> (IV. iv. 46 f.)

During his visit to the Greek camp Hector's fine talent for friendship and generosity expresses itself in gestures as well as words. 'Let me embrace thee, Ajax' (IV. v. 135), he cries, instead of making his opponent feel his superior fighting power and skill, and: 'The issue is embracement' (IV. v. 148). He offers him his hand with the words: 'Give me thy hand, my cousin' (IV. v. 157), and also the meeting with Nestor is accompanied by hearty embracements. To Nestor's: 'O, let an old man embrace thee' he responds with an enthusiastic: 'Let me embrace thee, good old chronicle' (IV. v. 202), and he repeats a moment later: 'Most reverend Nestor, I am glad to clasp thee.' We may note here in passing how constantly and in how many different ways the age of Nestor is mirrored in the speeches.

Direct naming can be replaced by a metaphorical reference to a gesture, endowing it with fuller significance. This happens where Hector lays down his sword with the words:

> Rest, sword; thou hast thy fill of blood and death!'
> (V. viii. 4)

and where Achilles describes the sheathing of his sword:

> My half-supp'd sword, that frankly would have fed,
> Pleas'd with this dainty bait, thus goes to bed.
> (V. viii. 19 f.)

There are two impulse words in this speech. 'This' demands a demonstrative look or gesture towards Hector's corpse, and 'thus' indicates the moment at which his sword must go into its place, suggesting at the same time the energy and precision of Achilles' action.

A rather interesting question is raised by a line addressed by Aeneas to himself as a warning against the vulgar and—in Shakespeare's play—typically Greek vice of self-praise:

> Peace, Troyan; lay thy finger on thy lips.
> (I. iii. 240)

It would be a mistake to consider this as a genuine mirror passage. The well-known gesture for demanding silence is introduced to give emphasis to Aeneas' warning to himself. It has the function of a metaphor; to realize it in action would most probably render it silly and ineffective.

Much more frequent than the self-descriptions with which we have dealt so far are references in one character's speech to the behaviour of another character. Before accosting Ulysses, Achilles says in front of his tent: 'Here is Ulysses. I'll interrupt his reading' (III. iii. 92 f.). The kissing-game in which the Greek leaders indulge after Cressida's arrival in their camp is consistently mirrored in speech. When Agamemnon begins it, his action is given importance and weight by Nestor's stately line:

Our general doth salute you with a kiss.
(IV. v. 19)

There is more subtlety in references to facial expression as we find one in Cressida's words to her lover when she does not want the early callers to find him in her house:

My lord, come you again into my chamber.
You smile and mock me, as if I meant naughtily.
(IV. ii. 36 f.)

The quality of Troilus' smile is thus precisely defined. The play-wright indicates, besides, that this mocking, and slightly salacious, smile develops into laughter by giving the young man's reaction as 'Ha! Ha!' What is evidently a rather bovine stare in Achilles makes Hector say:

Why dost thou so oppress me with thine eye?
(IV. v. 241)

Manners of speaking are further important subjects of mirror passages. When Pandarus begins with his comments on the returning warriors and his incessant allusions to the virtues of Troilus, Cressida finds it necessary to warn him: 'Speak not so loud' (I. ii. 178). A little later, as Troilus marches by at last, Pandarus' enthusiasm grows so loud that his niece hisses at him: 'Peace, for shame, peace!' (I. ii. 222). Early in her decisive meeting with Troilus, Cressida interrupts her first loving words to him before the wish that their happiness may last is formulated. Her courtly lover describes as 'pretty' what is really ominous: 'What makes this pretty abruption?' (III. ii. 62 f.). Pandarus' manner of opening his most painful interview with his niece is emphasized by her words: 'Why sigh you so profoundly?' (IV. ii. 79). The off-stage exclamation which announces Cassandra's first entrance is echoed by Priam: 'What noise, what shriek is this?' (II. ii. 97).

Silences, too, are rendered eloquent by spoken interpretation. Here Diomedes' aside on the reaction of Ajax to Ulysses' purposeful praise should be remembered:

> And how his silence drinks up this applause!
> (II. iii. 196)

Also Cressida's complaint to her lover:

> See, see, your silence,
> Cunning in dumbness, from my weakness draws
> My very soul of counsel. (III. ii. 128 ff.)

We may mention here that spoken references to sounds produced by instruments are also frequent in our play. Troilus' exclamation:

> Peace, you ungracious clamours! Peace, rude sounds!
> (I. i. 88)

which corresponds to the Q and F stage direction 'Sound alarum', is an instance of this; another occurs in I. iii. 256 f., where Aeneas' order:

> Trumpet, blow loud,
> Send thy brass voice through all these lazy tents;

is followed, at line 259, by 'Sound trumpet' in Q and by 'The trumpets sound' in F. After IV. v. 275, where Agamemnon commands:

> Beat loud the tabourines, let the trumpets blow,

there is no stage direction in either Q or F. This is certainly not a sign that the order was not executed; it is merely an example of the casual treatment of the stage directions in our texts. The lines we have quoted do service as spoken stage directions, but there is more to them, of course. Like many other mirror passages, they assist the imagination in its transmutation of stage effects into perfect elements of the dramatic world created by Shakespeare in and for the theatre of the mind. To say that the actual theatre with its human and material imperfections is subservient to the theatre of the mind is not to denigrate it. Its glory lies in the fact that, without it, the theatre of the mind cannot reach and hold Shakespeare's creation in its completeness and full vitality. The words in our last quotations give the possibly meagre and routine stage sounds their precise imaginative function, and they achieve this by their rhythm and their onomatopoeic qualities rather than by their plain meaning. A striking example of the transmutation of a trumpet call by a mirror passage occurs at the beginning of IV. v. Agamemnon, having referred to the 'appointment fresh and fair' in which Ajax hopes to overcome Hector, asks him to call the tardy Trojan to the lists:

> Give with thy trumpet a loud note to Troy,
> Thou dreadful Ajax, that the appalled air
> May pierce the head of the great combatant,
> And hale him hither. (IV. v. 3 ff.)

The invitation itself seems ironically attuned to the excessive and dull fortissimo which is the characteristic mode of Ajax and which appears presently with unsurpassable vehemence in his order to his trumpeter. Ajax's order transforms this good man into a grotesque caricature of his employment:

> Thou, trumpet, there's my purse.
> Now crack thy lungs and split thy brazen pipe;
> Blow, villain, till thy sphered bias cheek
> Out-swell the colic of puff'd Aquilon.
> Come, stretch thy chest, and let thy eyes spout blood:
> Thou blowest for Hector. (IV. v. 6 ff.)

By this extraordinary piece of rant the trumpet call which follows (again not mentioned in a stage direction) becomes the voice of Ajax's vainglorious pride.

No sounds have a more important function in the play than the knocks at the door that bring Troilus' and Cressida's first and only night of love to its disastrous close. There are three references to them in the text, suggesting that the impatient visitors knock more energetically each time they make themselves heard after their first attempt. Cressida is the first to react. She says:

> Who's that at door? Good uncle, go and see.
> (IV. ii. 35)

And a little later:

> How earnestly they knock! (IV. ii. 40)

The third mirror passage comes from Pandarus:

> Will you beat down the door? (IV. ii. 43)

The contrast between the hollow sounds, the meaning of which is known to the audience, and the frivolous conversation of Pandarus and the unsuspecting couple is a poignant dramatic effect. It makes this scene a worthy pendant to the knocking at the gate in *Macbeth*.

Returning to mirror passages that remain within the visual sphere, we wish to study a particularly interesting one, showing a habitual trick of behaviour. Ulysses recognizes Diomedes at a distance by his gait:

> 'Tis he, I ken the manner of his gait:
> He rises on the toe. That spirit of his
> In aspiration lifts him from the earth.
> (IV. v. 14 ff.)

The description of Diomedes' peculiarity is followed by an interpretation in terms of character. Other references to appearance are less decisive, but they all contribute something to our image of one of the dramatis personae. Hector hopes to recognize Achilles 'by his large and portly size' (IV. v. 162). Troilus' tribute to Cressida's fascinating eyes: 'Sleep kill those pretty eyes' (IV. ii. 4), is improved upon by Diomedes:

> The lustre in your eye, heaven in your cheek,
> Pleads your fair usage; (IV. iv. 117 f.).

From Ulysses, however, who is not among her lovers, comes the famous uncomplimentary interpretation of her charms:

> There's language in her eye, her cheek, her lip,
> Nay, her foot speaks; her wanton spirits look out
> At every joint and motive of her body. (IV. v. 55 ff.)

Moods and emotions, too, have their physical equivalents in appearance and gesture, and these appear in a number of mirror passages. Before the eagerly expected meeting with Cressida Troilus exclaims:

> I am giddy; expectation whirls me round.
> (III. ii. 17)

The corresponding condition in Cressida is mirrored by Pandarus before her entrance: 'She does so blush, and fetches her wind so short, as if she were fray'd with a sprite' (III. ii. 30). The depression of the two lovers after their separation is written on their faces. Achilles promises Cressida:

> I'll take that winter from your lips, fair lady,
> (IV. v. 24)

and Agamemnon inquires concerning Troilus:

> What Troyan is that same that looks so heavy?
> (IV. v. 95)

Besides its numerous short mirror passages our play contains a few complete mirror scenes, in which a whole series of stage events is described and interpreted. The first is the passing of the Trojan heroes before Pandarus and Cressida. Pandarus has his say concerning each of them, but his gabble does not mention many characteristic features. Hector's and Troilus' hacked helmets and Troilus' bloodied sword are noticed. Otherwise he offers no more than a lively general introduction of the Trojan lords, his talk being strictly subservient to his intention of whetting Cressida's interest in Troilus. In her subsequent soliloquy we find the lines:

> But more in Troilus thousand-fold I see
> Than in the glass of Pandar's praise may be,
> (I. ii. 276 f.)

Although mainly an avowal of secret passion, they are also a criticism of Pandarus' superficial talk, and they contain a beautiful phrase foreshadowing our own more prosaic and technical terms 'mirror passage' and 'mirror scene'.

Another mirror scene, the fight between Hector and Ajax, was evidently executed according to well-known conventions. The mirror words (IV. v. 113 ff.) throw light on a few incidents of the fight only. A more intimate and individualized scene like the bringing together of the lovers by Pandarus is mirrored in much greater detail. The following speech is replete with mirror elements as well as with gestic impulses for the speaker himself:

> Come, come, what need you blush? Shame's a baby.—Here she is now; swear the oaths now to her that you have sworn to me.—What, are you gone again? You must be watch'd ere you be made tame, must you? Come your ways, come your ways; and you draw backward, we'll put you i' th' fills.—Why do you not speak to her?—Come, draw this curtain and let's see your picture. Alas the day, how loath you are to offend daylight! An 'twere dark, you'd close sooner. So, so; rub on, and kiss the mistress. . . . (III. ii. 39 ff.)

The amusing scene in which the Greek princes pass by Achilles without showing the customary signs of respect is first described by Ulysses when he arranges it

> Achilles stands i' th' entrance of his tent.
> Please it our general pass strangely by him,
> As if he were forgot; and, Princes all,
> Lay negligent and loose regard upon him.
> (III. iii. 38 ff.)

Presently, the plan is executed before our eyes, and Patroclus describes what is happening in the very words of Ulysses: 'They pass by strangely' (III. iii. 71). And Achilles, looking back on the scene, complains to Ulysses:

> they pass'd by me
> As misers do by beggars—neither gave to me
> Good word nor look. (III. iii. 142 ff.)

Thus, by repetition, the significance of the scene as a whole is emphasized; and the behaviour of the princes is precisely defined by the allusions to their way of looking and speaking and by Achilles' striking simile.

The most complex use of the mirror technique is found in V. ii. It has its functions in the would-be-secret conversation between Cressida and Diomedes. His reactions appear in some of Cressida's speeches:

> Nay, but you part in anger. (V. ii. 44)

> You look upon that sleeve; behold it well (V. ii. 68)

> Nay, do not snatch it from me; (V. ii. 80).

> One cannot speak a word
> But it straight starts you. (V. ii, 99 f.)

The speeches of Troilus, the tormented watcher, are another mirror of what is going on before Calchas' tent. Two of them are quite simple. The statement 'Cressid comes forth to him' (V. ii. 6) is uttered with the accent of one refusing to believe what his eyes are seeing. The four words 'She strokes his cheek' (V. ii. 51), mirroring the fact so dryly and objectively, are probably the most concentrated and intense expression of passion and suffering in the whole play. These two bare mirror speeches are more heartrending than any of Troilus' later violent outbreaks with all their powerful rhetoric. There are further mirror effects in Troilus' reactions upon the disastrous scene: the whispering which follows upon Cressida's 'Hark, a word with you' (V. ii. 7) provokes Troilus' 'Yea, so familiar!' (V. iii. 8). Her: 'Hark! a word in your ear.' (V. ii. 34) is followed by his outcry: 'O plague and madness!' We may add here that Troilus' is not the only viewpoint from which the events before the tent are seen. Thersites, too, is lurking in the dark and snarling forth the lowest possible interpretations of Cressida's behaviour. When she says:

I prithee, Diomed, visit me no more,

he fears that this could be mistaken for the voice of her better nature and comments:

Now she sharpens. Well said, whetstone. (V. ii. 74)

The third great mirror effect of this amazing multiple scene is found in Ulysses' remarks on the reactions of Troilus. His first speech (V. ii. 5) places the watchers. He has then his own not too kindly remark on Cressida ('She will sing any man at first sight'— V. ii. 9), but, before long, he realizes the folly of adding fuel to Troilus' passion, the growth of which is reflected in what he says in order to keep the young man reasonably quiet:

You are moved, Prince; let us depart, I pray, (V. ii. 36).

You flow to great distraction; (V. ii. 41).

You shake, my lord, at something; will you go? (V. ii, 50)

The complex system of mirror effects, together with the numerous gestic impulses contained in the speeches, gives the scene before us its three-dimensional reality and its intense dramatic power. Any adequate performance of it must be based on this system and these hints. They cannot be slurred over or ignored for the sake of an 'original' conception of the play by a producer who has grasped our great author-producer's method of expressing his total vision in dramatic speech. There is a legitimate sphere for the new producer's originality. Shakespeare's theatrical notation is anything but pedantic. It is precise and definite in certain crucial situations; far more often it is allusive and suggestive. Once they have been caught and understood, there are many different ways of realizing the author's suggestions on the stage. In their realization the talents of new producers and actors and the spirit of a new age should manifest themselves.

We cannot include in this paper a study of the numerous gestic impulses in our text, although, without it, our account of the theatrical physiognomy of *Troilus and Cressida* remains a fragment. But we must devote the rest of the space at our disposal to the reported scenes. In these the characters seen on the real stage appear in additional scenes on the stage of the mind, their behaviour entirely controlled by the author himself. As our first example hesitates between a simple report and a reported scene it is advisable to define the difference between the two forms. In a report we obtain information on facts and events as causes or consequences of other facts and events, on the results of what people think, say, and do; the reported scene on the other hand is concerned with action in progress, with the behaviour, the very words of people in a particular situation. It has a tendency to change from the past to the present tense, and it definitely prefers direct to indirect speech. Here is Alexander's report on Hector's anger:

> Hector, whose patience
> Is as a virtue fix'd, to-day was mov'd.
> He chid Andromache, and struck his armourer;
> And, like as there were husbandry in war,
> Before the sun rose he was harness'd light,
> And to the field goes he; . . . . (I. ii. 4 ff.)

Only the last line achieves the immediacy of the reported scene. Our next example shows much more of this quality. It is Pandarus' account of the frivolous conversation at the Trojan court, in the course of which Helena tries to make fun of Troilus because there are so few hairs on his chin as yet, and finds his wit rather more than a match for her own. This account is itself the subject of a frivolous conversation, in which Pandarus cleverly stimulates Cressida's love for Troilus by making her a little jealous. He paints a charming scene of the easy-going life of the Trojan princes when they forget about the war. His reported scene supports the effect of a later acted scene (III. i.) where Pandarus and Helena converse in the same tone. Besides, it adds important touches to our experience of Troilus, whom we never see in a similar situation on the stage.

The most striking reported scene of the play, however, shows how Achilles wastes his time while he is withholding his strength from the Greek cause. It has its place in Ulysses' great speech before the Greek council of war. By way of contrast and relief it introduces gesture, movement, and action into a speech and a scene predominantly rhetorical. In the corresponding situation in the Trojan council of war the irruption of Cassandra has a similar function. The scene presented by Ulysses (I. iii. 142 ff.) has a setting (the tent with 'a lazy bed'), a protagonist ('great Achilles', 'large Achilles', 'god Achilles', 'Sir Valour') and a second actor, Patroclus. He amuses his friend by a parodistic imitation of Agamemnon's gait and speech and of Nestor's way of getting ready for a public oration and of responding to a night alarm. Patroclus' imitation is mostly gestic. When he 'pageants' Agamemnon he walks in the silly, self-important way of a ham-actor—Ulysses makes this clear by his detailed theatrical simile. His impersonation of Nestor includes hemming and beard-stroking, coughing, spitting and 'palsy-fumbling on his gorget'. Achilles, though 'on his press'd bed lolling', is no passive spectator of the fun. His applause and laughter are loud, and he keeps giving new promising tasks to his talented entertainer. Some of the finest points of the whole wonderful passage spring from the fact that both Agamemnon and Nestor are among Ulysses' audience. Thus we can compare Patroclus' imitations to their originals, and are certainly not expected to find them as weak as Ulysses makes them appear in his suspiciously over-emphatic disclaimers.

Our image of Ajax, too, is derived from many sources besides his own actions and speeches on the stage. Alexander describes his character to Cressida (I. ii. 18 ff.); in the council scene Nestor tells of his behaviour under the influence of Achilles' bad example (I. iii. 188 ff.). There are references to 'blockish Ajax', 'dull brainless Ajax' when Ulysses and Nestor are hatching their plot of rousing Achilles from his inactivity by pretending that Ajax is the proper match for Hector. Thus his first entrance on the stage does not find us unprepared. In II. iii, where Ulysses and his friends gleefully feed his illusion that he is Achilles' better, we get further characterizing strokes in the contemptuous asides of the watchers. The results of Ulysses' and Nestor's cajolery are the subject of an amusing reported scene coming from Thersites in III. iii: 'Ajax goes up and down the field asking for himself.' '. . . he raves in saying nothing.' 'Why, 'a stalks up and down like a peacock—a stride and a stand; ruminates like an hostess that hath no arithmetic but her brain to set down her reckoning, bites his lip with a politic regard. . . .' (III. iii. 245 ff.) Gestures and behaviour are given life and precision by a series of telling similes. When the image of the stalking *miles gloriosus* is fully alive before our imagination, Thersites is struck by the idea of supplementing his reported scene by an acted one, in which he takes the part of Ajax. Through an astonishingly resourceful combination of mirror effects Ajax is shown from many different angles, and becomes a character expressing itself in behaviour as well as speech.

Similarly, our experience of Hector receives a number of important modifications in reported scenes. In IV. v., his qualities as an invincible fighter and generous victor are appreciated by Nestor in a speech that is particularly impressive because it is the tribute of an enemy. His clemency towards a vanquished opponent appears a second time in Troilus' lines:

> When many times the captive Grecian falls,
> Even in the fan and wind of your fair sword,
> You bid them rise and live. (V. iii. 40 ff.)

Like Nestor's tribute, this speech represents a type of reported scene removed from actuality by the fact that it describes habitual action. Nestor's report on Hector's activity in his last battle is different. It has all the force of a spectator's reaction upon what he sees:

> There is a thousand Hectors in the field;
> Now here he fights on Galathe his horse,
> And there lacks work; anon he's there afoot,
> And there they fly or die, like scaled sculls
> Before the belching whale ... (V. v. 19 ff.)

A reported scene may also introduce the dimension of the future into a play. Cressida, in IV. ii, having vented her grief before our eyes, speaks of the more violent demonstrations that are to follow in her room:

> I'll go in and weep—
> ... Tear my bright hair, and scratch my praised cheeks,
> Crack my clear voice with sobs and break my heart,
> With sounding 'Troilus'. (IV. ii. 104 ff.)

A different future scene, which takes us beyond the time limits of the play, is reported by Cassandra when she adds her prophecy of doom to her family's endeavours to prevent Hector from joining the battle on the fateful day:

> O, farewell, dear Hector!
> Look how thou diest. Look how thy eye turns pale.
> Look how thy wounds do bleed at many vents.
> Hark how Troy roars; how Hecuba cries out.
> (V. iii. 80 ff.)

Her mantic gift shows her the coming scenes as present and real. By her prophecy the spectator is attuned to the horror and the historic importance of Hector's death, so that the actual death scene can be passed over rather rapidly. After the event the effect of the unhappy news on the Trojans appears in Troilus' words:

> There is a word will Priam turn to stone;
> Make wells and Niobes of the maids and wives,
> Cold statues of the youth; and, in a word,
> Scare Troy out of itself. (V. x. 18 ff.)

Here, no realistic scene is described. The extreme despair of the Trojans is expressed by a series of hyperbolical images. The cessation of movement in Priam and the youth of Troy becomes a powerful symbol. This passage is a good example to show how gesture, so essential a direct means of expression in our play, also pervades its imagery. In this sphere innumerable playlets are enacted before our inner eye by personifications and metamorphosed abstractions. They occur frequently within the speeches, which interrupt the course of events and form a fascinating contrast to the many gestic and bustling scenes. The gestic imagery, again, keeps the highly rhetorical and sententious speeches within the stylistic framework of the rest of the play. 'Time', in Ulysses' exhortation to Achilles,

> hath, my lord, a wallet at his back,
> Wherein he puts alms for oblivion,
> A great-siz'd monster of ingratitudes.
> (III. iii. 145 ff.)

It assumes another part in the same speech:

> For Time is like a fashionable host,
> That slightly shakes his parting guest by th' hand;
> And with his arms outstretch'd, as he would fly,
> Grasps in the comer. (III, iii. 165 ff.)

For Troilus, at the parting,

> Injurious time now with a robber's haste
> Crams his rich thievery up, he knows not how.
> As many farewells as be stars in heaven,
> With distinct breath and consign'd kisses to them,
> He fumbles up into a loose adieu.
> (IV. iv. 41 ff.)

These examples suffice to show how indispensable the gestic mode of apprehension and expression was for the author of *Troilus and Cressida*. It is this mode which made him the supreme dramatist. The desire to learn as much as possible about its manifestations in the texts should animate the critics as well as the producers and actors of Shakespeare. It can take them to a common ground where the line of demarcation mentioned in the opening paragraph of this paper may be profitably discussed.

VI

The Speaking of Shakespeare's Verse

GUY BOAS

THERE is no tradition of acting Shakespeare in England. No visitor from overseas coming to this country can count on seeing a Shakespearian production of the certain excellence which one of Molière or Racine by the Comédie Française would attain in Paris. The visitor may attend a West End performance of Shakespeare and see something which is splendid, mediocre, or feeble. He may go to the provinces, to a school or village hall, he may watch a stage anywhere in the British Isles, in or out of doors, he may patronize professionals or amateurs, adults or children, yet he never knows and, neither do we natives ever know, whether we are going to see the plays of the greatest dramatist glorified, competently presented, or murdered.

So far as most good professional casts are concerned this is not the same with modern plays or with prose classics. West End production is usually admirable, and one comes away from witnessing a performance of Farquhar, Sheridan, Shaw, Somerset Maugham, or Terence Rattigan, thinking that this could hardly have been done better, and envying the skill of all concerned. Critics often criticize the play but have usually little but praise for the acting.

With Shakespeare, however, it is quite otherwise. The average cultivated member of the audience is rarely stirred to enthusiasm, is often eloquent on shortcomings and, even if he does not say much, leaves the theatre with a strange, almost subconscious sense of dissatisfaction: it was not what he wanted, or what he liked; he had gone to see one of the great plays of the world, and somehow he suspects that he has only seen it through a glass darkly. He does not know what was wrong (that is not his business), but he feels he has been cheated of his vision, and he begins to wonder whether, after all, Charles Lamb was not wise in preferring to read *King Lear* to seeing it acted upon a stage.

Occasionally a star brings off a real achievement, such as Godfrey Tearle as Othello, Leon Quartermain as Mercutio, Gielgud as Benedick, Olivier as Richard III, Michael Hordern as Menenius, Vanessa Redgrave as Rosalind. This list is not exhaustive, but often disappointment is in proportion to the distinction of the star, and where the star shines but the minor parts are indifferently played the total effect is marred.

What is the reason for this mystery? Our country has produced the greatest dramatist of all time. Since the days of Dryden Shakespeare's fame has steadily conquered the world, and at no time have his plays been more eagerly watched, and been more sincerely admired than they are today. What evil fairy has stolen into the festival and jeopardized any certainty that we can see an adequate performance?

In the first place Shakespeare's plays suffer on the stage because they are so well known. It is not merely that the audience are comparing an actor or actress with a greater one whom they have seen in the part before, but because every lover of Shakespeare has in his mind's eye an ideal conception of the protagonists. If you have always felt Hamlet to be a thrilling, shining, brilliant, kaleidoscopic prince, passing from one mood to another with incandescent temperamental impulse, at one moment mocking Polonius, at another upbraiding the Queen, ridiculing Osric, unburdening his soul in honest friendship to Horatio, defying the Ghost, instructing the players, wrestling and duelling with Laertes, and, after in a final frenzy of action slaying Claudius, passing from the world with the loveliest classical diction on his lips, you will not be satisfied with a presentation of his character, however accomplished, which is merely a sombre and morbid portrayal of a gloomy Dane. You looked, in your mind's eye, for life and speed and movement but you were given slow academic philosophy, you looked for colour but you were led only through fog. If you picture Othello the soul of magnanimity you will not be satisfied with merely a jealous coloured mercenary. If your conception of Bottom is of a poor head but a warm, spacious heart you will not like only a clown; if Caliban means to you the pathos of the elemental savage, you will not relish a tipsy golliwog.

That is why Lamb found Shakespeare's conception of *Lear*, evolved from his imagination of the world delivered back into chaos, with the King's mind representing, like Prometheus, humanity writhing in torment, so far exceeded what it is possible for the average producer to present on a platform with human players and painted scenery that he preferred out of his own sensibilities to follow Shakespeare mentally rather than let contortions of puppets come between him and the awe-inspiring conception.

Next to be noted is that Shakespearian casts are very large ones. It is expensive enough to pay a moderate cast to play Shakespeare; to pay for a good one, a good producer, and good costumes is costly indeed: and, while enthusiasm for Shakespeare among audiences is now great, there is no guarantee of support for long runs. The longest run in the history of the British theatre is *The Mousetrap*—over 4,000 performances: the next two longest are those of *Salad Days*—2,283 performances; and *Chu-Chin-Chow*—2,238. The longest Shakespearian run is that of Irving's *Merchant of Venice* which was given at the Lyceum on 250 occasions. While the capital invested in *My Fair Lady* or *Oliver!* can be counted on bringing in a return of income for years, who is going to get an adequate return on producing *Measure for Measure* or *Troilus and Cressida*?

Lastly there is the question of fashion. A theatre audience is not composed only of one generation. Today it still includes a few who admired the Victorian productions of Irving and Ellen Terry, the middle-aged who thrilled to the magnificence of Shakespeare embellished at His Majesty's by Tree, those just old enough to remember the thrill of Gielgud in his pristine vigour at the Old Vic, and those who have come to see Shakespeare with shining eyes for the first time. Those who enjoy Olivier would now probably find Irving 'ham', while those who have been moved by Irving's dynamic genius or Lewis Waller's elocution or Gielgud's diction find the frequent prosaic restraint and offhand delivery of modern players pale and insipid. We still ask why there appears to be no standard, no norm. Why are we perpetually at the mercy of each new venture in production to which we go not confidently but as to an experiment?

Shakespeare's work was produced under the specific conditions of the Elizabethan theatre: and two of these were of special importance. Firstly the theatre was small, the stage projected into the audience, and the actor with the audience thus round him could speak poetry at intimate close-quarters. He could set up a circular electric and psychological current far more easily than can be done in the modern playhouse, where he only faces his audience—usually over an orchestral pit and sometimes with a big area to permeate in the case of the larger houses. Secondly, female roles in Elizabethan days were played by boys.

Shakespeare is the first of dramatists but also he is psychologist and poet. It is this trilogy of gifts which has made adequate playing of him so difficult. The normal being cannot appreciate more than one art medium at a time. Wagner's ideal in music-drama of music equal with words and words equal with music and scenery equal with both is perfect in theory. But in practice an audience cannot absorb all three elements simultaneously. If one is fully absorbing the music, one cannot pay full attention to dialogue: if one is admiring Lohengrin's swan or Brunnhilde's horse or the battlements of Klingsor's castle or the flames which envelop Valhalla, one cannot also be spotting *leit-motifs* in the orchestra or appreciating the force of Wotan's conversation.

So with Shakespeare we are faced with a paradox. His sense of theatre was so sustained that something dramatic is almost always taking place—Kent is put in the stocks, Orlando and Charles wrestle, Iachimo creeps from the trunk, Shylock whets his knife, Desdemona drops her handkerchief, Falstaff is covered with dirty linen, and, when there seems no means of getting rid of him otherwise, Antigonus is chased out by a bear. Now while such incidents are taking place we are constantly required to absorb transcendent poetic speech. How is this to be done, or rather, how can the player help us to do so?

Abt Vogler's definition of music—the producing of 'not a

fourth sound, but a star' explains the setting up of those overtones and undertones which we all recognize in authentic poetry. It is not a question of the technicalities of verse, which only amount to rhythm being regularly recurrent. We may get poetry in prose as easily as in verse, for it is not a matter of a sequence of iambic pentameters but of certain chemicals in the poet which create the magic. Is there much less poetry in the prose of Hamlet than in his blank verse? 'If it be now, tis not to come; if it be not to come, it will be now; if it be not now, yet it will come: the readiness is all.' Othello touches the poetic heights in

> But I do love thee! And when I love thee not
> Chaos is come again.
>
> (III. iii. 92–3)

But Desdemona equally attains them in her cry of faith to Emilia, 'I do not think there is any such woman.'

Poetry is not essential to the theatre. Greek tragedy was poetry, but the plays of Aeschylus and Sophocles were not theatrical but religious. Elizabethan drama was poetic because poetry was the natural expression of the era, of a piece with the romantic exploits of the men of action who served under the spell of the Virgin Queen. But poetry is not inseparable from the writing of great plays or the plays of Molière and Ibsen would not be master-pieces. Poetry may be the final glory in drama, but it is distinct in kind from the other ingredients: moreover it is far from certain that the playhouse is the ideal place in which to appreciate it. A quiet voice reading aloud to two or three listeners at home may provide better conditions in which to catch the magic of the most exacting of the arts because it contains not only sound and colour but also thought.

How then is the actor to cope? The part of the boy player on the Elizabethan stage takes us to the heart of the matter. Pro-fessor Raleigh in his *Shakespeare* writes, 'It may be doubted whether Shakespeare has not suffered more than he has gained by the genius of latter-day actors, who bring into plays a realism and robust emotion which sometimes obscure the sheer poetic value of the author's conception. . . . Poetry, like religion, is outraged when it is made a platform for the exhibition of their own talent and passion by those who are its ministers.'

Perhaps no boy can be expected to act with perfect histrionic gesticulation and movement the passion and progress of Cleopatra through the three hours' traffic of her ascending tragedy. But inversely an actress who attempts to give this display is in danger of failing to convey all that Shakespeare has to say in poetry which from the fourth act onwards soars into the empyrean. An accomplished actress may give an exciting theatrical performance, but if she does so she probably will not give an equally satisfying poetic performance, not because she may not herself appreciate the poetry, but because human receptivity cannot take in the two elements at one and the same time.

Is it chance that the supreme effect wrought on the audience in the Queen's part are the final words when, crowned and enthroned, she is sitting motionless with the asp nearby?

> Give me my robe, put on my crown; I have
> Immortal longings in me . . .
> I am fire and air; my other elements
> I give to baser life.
>
> (V. ii. 278-87)

In performance it is not only that Shakespeare here rises to an apex, but that the player is bound to sit at rest facing the audience and has no temptation to do anything but speak to them. So Shakespeare's words can cast their full spell, and perhaps for the first time during the evening we feel that the poet is speaking to us face to face, and is not merely a voice rising from the play's relentless action.

Lear's sublime raving may easily produce less effect than when Kent confined in the stocks, half murmurs in soliloquy as he falls asleep,

> All weary and o'erwatched,
> Take vantage, heavy eyes, not to behold
> This shameful lodging.

Fortune goodnight; smile once more; turn thy wheel.

(II. ii. 165–8)

Bolingbroke utters many a splendid fighting speech as gradually he filches the crown and drives the feeble Richard to Pomfret, but never exerts that mesmeric hold as when sitting exhausted by insomnia, as monarch he unburdens himself in solitary weakness and remorse:

How many thousand of my poorest subjects
Are at this hour asleep! . . .
Uneasy lies the head that wears a crown.

(III. i. 4–31)

Should there then be no movement; nothing but speech? Were that so, Shakespeare need never have written for the theatre, and we might as well sit at home and read his text. What must be devised is a balance whereby histrionics do not intervene between the author's poetry and the audience's imagination. In the case of that rare player, the natural and perfect Shakespearian, the balance will be achieved spontaneously, but for normal capability some principle must be set down. Gesture and motion should proceed *from* the words, to illustrate and enhance, but they must not interfere or supersede. All movement must be in relation to the sense, economical or non-existent when the words demand it, and never so extravagant as to overtop even rhetoric when it occurs. And tempo is everything. A Shakespearian play is like an orchestral score. A curve should cover the sequent lines and passages, with a major curve covering the whole act, and another starting from the first word of the play, rising over the whole action and completing itself by falling in gradual cadence onto the final syllable of act five.

Only by thinking thus in terms of music can proper justice be done to poetic drama. Action in Shakespeare must accommodate itself to rhythm. Only when they are fused can they produce their perfect reflection of the rhythm of nature.

The boy actor fits this particular task and surmounts instinctively the particular difficulties by acting, more easily than can an adult, purely as a medium through whom Shakespeare can speak.

In prose plays where personality counts supremely the adult with
that quality naturally excels. But when Shakespearian verse is
spoken personality easily becomes an obstacle. A struggle sets in
between the actor and the poet and the greater the fascination
which the actor's personality normally exerts, the more difficult
is it to let the poetry make its effect. The personalities of some of
the best actors would be wasted in Shakespeare, for as they do not
suit poetry, Shakespeare does not suit them.

Those who have watched Greek plays at Bradfield know how
impressive they are. One comes away feeling that one has been
in direct touch with the poet. No especial praise is due to the
boys for any extraordinary stage ability. It is, indeed, because
they are *not* trained actors that they play their parts so well. Provided they move with dignity, speak with intelligence and sin-
cerity and with that beauty of vocal tone so often found in boys of
that age, all is well, and their very lack of artifice is a blessing.

How then should professional producers and players of Shakespeare set about their task? Probably the best advice which could
be given them would be that they should think of the plays in
terms of music, and if they are unable to do so they should leave
Shakespeare alone.

Let the play be thought of as a symphony, as a feast of sound as
well as sense—just as music to the initiated is a product of intellect
as well as emotion. Let the producer assume the garment of a
conductor as well as his own. Let him recognize, and see that his
players recognize, that the passages of verse have each their appropriate tempo—allegretto, andante, largo, presto, as in music. He
must see the crescendos and diminuendos are observed, sfor-
zandos and rallentandos, that here the passage is written in the
mood of scherzando (the badinage of Beatrice and Benedick),
there allegro agitato (Hamlet railing at Ophelia), presto feroce
(Hamlet in the grave storming at Laertes), allegro brutale (Lear's
curses), andante cantabile ('If music be the food of love, play on'),
andante calmo (Othello before the Senate), sostenuto e grave
(Lear: 'Blow winds, and crack your cheeks'), presto con agita-
zione (Edgar's feigned madness), lento tragico (Shylock leaves
the court), sforzando tragico (Malvolio: 'I'll be revenged on the

whole pack of you'), and what better direction for Rosalind than allegretto con vivacita?

Also let there be recognized that the plays seem to contain their concerted vocal numbers as well as their solos: the trio, for instance, in the graveyard scene of Horatio (baritone), First Gravedigger (bass-buffo), with Hamlet (tenor) soaring up the scale to high notes of nervous climax: 'Let her paint an inch thick, to this favour she must come; make her laugh at that.' Or again, the wonderful quintet in *Troilus and Cressida* in which the agonized Troilus (tenor) with Ulysses (bass) watch from the wings Cressida and Diomede centre stage (soprano and baritone), with Thersites (counter-tenor) uttering a mocking obbligato from the opposite corner.

The great ensembles are obvious; sometimes sombre—the banquet scene in *Macbeth*, the opening scene of *Lear*, the assassination of Caesar in the Capitol, or sometimes radiant—*Pyramus and Thisbe* played before Theseus and the court, the banquet on Pompey's galley, or the masked ball in *Romeo and Juliet*. These should be treated as Bernard Shaw rehearsed his own prose dramas when he directed that the voices should follow one another, clash, or intermingle, as instruments of an orchestra.

Of course the analogy is not precise, the producer is dealing with words and not with music, but if he remembers that he is dealing with verbal music as well as verbal sense, and carries the idea of music in his mind, an essence will emerge, and a continuity be preserved, in which all questions of the managing of metre by the players will resolve themselves and come right without any selfconscious or tedious attention to metrical or poetic technique, and at last, like the sun emerging from behind the clouds, the full glory of the plays will be apparent.

Shakespeare's constant references to music, and the fact that so many of his scenes call for incidental music, show that music as well as poetry possessed his soul, and unless, therefore, that music is extracted when he is performed, the effect is lacking as much as when a composer's score is only read in the study.

At present this truth is demonstrated only by chance. One or two players only in a cast may speak so as to produce the spell.

Sometimes a player produces it for a speech or two and then the music dies away. Sometimes it comes from the voice of a quite minor character so that though the protagonist never plays the tune, his servant in a line or two does suddenly give us the melody. Whether one hears the music uttered by a star or by an adult amateur or by a schoolboy is unpredictable for, except in the case of rare professional players, one can never be sure that one will hear the music until it happens. And the 'pity of it, Iago', because there are few professionals or amateurs who couldn't understand the secret and produce the right result if only they were shown. Far more people have good speaking voices than even they know themselves, provided they are shown how to use them and are not afraid to do so. It is no question of 'vocalization', nor of any artificial speaking. The only method required is deep breathing (as in singing) so that the vocal cords receive sufficient breath, whether the passage be loud or soft, for their natural tone to be sustained, with all harshness eliminated by relaxation of the facial muscles. The music can then be played, but only if it is realized in the mind that the music is there to *be* played.

In the modern reaction against dramatic exuberance in favour of subdued realism in dialogue, nothing has been more unfortunate than the effect on the playing of Shakespeare, whose splendour can never fully return to the stage until producers and players have not only the intellect and imagination to portray his characters, but also the courage and confidence to give to his language the same controlled but unrestricted utterance that one expects from the player or singer of music. 'The man that hath no music in himself . . . Let no such man be trusted,' says Lorenzo. Certainly he cannot be trusted to act or produce Shakespeare.

VII

Shakespeare: The Actor's Problem

LAURENCE KITCHIN

THE scope of this subject is determined by two events: by the ending of the Old Vic's tenancy of the New Theatre in 1949 and by the setting up of the National Theatre in 1963. The first brought to an end the partnership of two great actors, Olivier and Richardson, working under favourable conditions not found again until the summer of 1962 when Olivier conducted his own season at Chichester. The second event amounted to an underwriting of those conditions by the Government and the London County Council. Essentially the conditions are a product of subsidy, repertory and a concentration of artistic forces. At the start of the period they also applied to the Gielgud-Ashcroft seasons at the Haymarket and at the close of it to the Royal Shakespeare's expansion. Although these were initially private ventures, attached to Littler and the Tennent organization, the assumption behind them was the same. The classics, including Shakespeare, can no longer be expected to pay for themselves.

It may seem a long way from these complex issues of finance to the critical appreciation of Shakespearian acting. That task might seem to begin at the moment the first lines are spoken and the audience settles down. For inter-war critics it effectively did. There would be actors on view who were known to have served their apprenticeship with Tree, Benson or Granville-Barker; innovations took place against a reasonably stable background. They could be identified readily and defined at length. James Agate, for example, had space enough to tell you what Benson had done with a passage in *Richard II* before reporting on a newcomer to the part. He also applied specific tests of skill, one of which was Othello's reaction to the drunken brawl:

Cassio, I love thee;
But never more be officer of mine . . .
Look if my gentle love be not rais'd up.
I'll make thee an example.

(II. iii. 240–3)

One can think of few critics more remote than Agate from the close-analysis school, yet here he was in touch with it, equally aware of the changes of tone and emotion in the passage quoted. Apart from the pounding severity of the second line, it is not remarkable as verse. Its quality is in the interplay of Othello's feelings, worn on his sleeve as usual and manipulated by Iago, who has staged the entire incident like an expert author directing his own work. Method acting, incapable of rhetoric or sublimity, would be quite in place here, not only for Othello, but for Iago and Cassio, too. But how can useful criticism of such an episode come about if there is no room to quote? Ban quotation, either for reasons of space or in deference to a journalistic fashion for jaunty writing, and you discard the main point of reference, the true focus of judgement, the text. From there it is a short step to favouring sets, costumes, or the directors 'ruling idea', factors more easily dealt with in a brief report. Where Agate's point of reference was Shakespeare's words, interpreted by the latest of a line of actors lodged in the memory for comparison, the reality of post-war dramatic criticism is often a journalist besieging the theatre's press officer in order to find out why *Much Ado about Nothing* has been dressed for the early nineteenth century. At its crudest this approach is summed up by a hasty question in the first interval: 'What's the gimmick?' Long before the first lines are spoken and while the audience is filing in, the gimmick may already have announced itself from the uncurtained set. It may well take three hours to decide on its merits and these may distract attention from nuances of acting, like the cordite in *Henry V in Battledress* (Mermaid, 1960). Nor will the actors have a training background as narrowly Shakespearian as that of the Bensonians. James Booth, the Royal Shakespeare Edmund of 1962, was dressed in tight trousers resembling jeans. His best known performances had been as a Soho spiv and an R.A.F. cook.

'I am resentful if criticism is uninformed or dismissive,' Peter Hall has said. 'After all, it is the only record of our work.' During the period under survey it has been a hasty and superficial record. Shakespearian acting has thus been deprived of one of its most valuable encouragements and supports. So much, that one has to remind oneself what its function is. It is to perform Shakespeare's plays in the medium they were written for, that is, live theatre, not films, television, radio or on disc, though all these substitutes have their uses. Parts like Hamlet, Antony, Cleopatra, Macbeth, Othello and Falstaff demand a range of expression rarely to be found in any one person. They are so exacting that the history of great interpreters is a history of incomplete successes, yet even partial success can illuminate the plays in a manner unknown to study of the written words. And in addition to the heroic central figures, the plays require large casts, the least of whom may find himself given a line of major poetry. To build a company of strength enough to satisfy both the major and minor acting demands would take more time and money than has ever been spent on the performing of Shakespeare in England. The business of star actors is to embody the Hamlets, Antonys and Othellos and to convey the magnificent language assigned them; the business of the others is to understand and further the grand design of each play. This unity of solo work and ensemble, this collective expression of riches obvious in the text, demands a concentration of artistic forces.

Under the pressure of war a hint of the ideal concentration was given by the New and Haymarket seasons. Gielgud, Olivier, Redgrave, Evans, Ashcroft, and Richardson were seen to be the greatest collection of Shakespearian actors within living memory. Then, after a few years of peace, dispersal began. With the rocketing of West End land values, speculators evicted the artists unless their terms were met, and their terms were the bad old inter-war terms, worst of all the long run, the relentless squeezing of profit from a success. Another was the toleration of Shakespeare under the imprint of star names on a budget too low for proper casting of other parts. A third was the assemblage and dismissal of *ad hoc* companies, to the detriment of group acting. Yet a fourth, scarcely noticed, was the promiscuous camping in different theatre buildings, none of which had time to acquire Shakespearian identity as the New had managed to do. Between 1946 and 1953 *Antony and Cleopatra* was produced at the Piccadilly, the Prince's and the St. James'. One result of the haphazard muddling through was the exclusion of great performances from the capital city. Gielgud's Angelo, Redgrave's Lear and Olivier's Macbeth had one thing in common; either you made the journey to Stratford-on-Avon or you never saw them at all.

The stars met this reactionary threat to their wartime glory by compromising with a situation loaded in favour of the speculator. They could earn enough money on the films or in entertainment pieces to force Shakespeare into the West End from time to time, into such theatres as were not held by long-running musicals, thrillers or farces. They could insist on limited runs, but no longer on repertory, supposedly disliked by the public, though it had filled the New and the Haymarket a few years before and was accepted eagerly for opera and the ballet. What they could not achieve was continuity, a secure foothold and a permanent company. None of them could afford to buy or build a theatre, and without that all efforts to stabilize the situation were doomed. The artistic needs of great actors, the cultural needs of a newly educated public, the country's prestige, as well as any duty owed to Shakespeare himself, all came lower in the scale of priorities than the profits to be milked from a few square feet of land in Central London. Symptomatic of this blinkered materialism was the reluctance of successive governments to disgorge the money earmarked for the National Theatre. We are dealing with cultural, not political priorities, it should be emphasized. Attempts were repeatedly made to defend the fitful and half-hearted commercial exploitation of Shakespeare. First, by pointing to achievements like Gielgud's Benedick, Ashcroft's Beatrice and Olivier's Titus, all mounted outside London originally. In relation to the talent existing, these were mere glimpses. Second, in justification was the vicious fallacy, so convenient to speculators, that actors are rogues and vagabonds who wilt in security. This argument, which makes sense to a cynical employer exploiting a surplus of labour, lost its teeth when applied to titled actors of world renown. It acted as a brake on progress, however, especially when allied to another fallacy which seeks to deny actors any skill in practical affairs.

Such degrading philistinism in an age of affluence was peculiar to England and, in England, peculiar to the drama, Shakespeare included. It did not apply to opera and the ballet, both munificently subsidized. One day the causes may be traced, perhaps discovered as far back as the closing of the theatres in 1642. Its effect on the acting of Shakespeare in the nineteen-fifties was simple. Great acting was rationed when an unprecedented number of admittedly great actors were in their prime. To cite homely examples, which most people interested in the subject can parallel, I was abroad on active service at the time of Richardson's Falstaff (New, 1945). I have still not seen it, because it has not been repeated, not once in eighteen years, though it is widely claimed to be the best of our time. Nor have I seen the growth of Olivier's Macbeth since the version he did under Saint-Denis (New, 1937), later perfected but never shown to London, not even as a film, for the projected Rank Organization production was shelved. Such are the results when definitive performances are at the mercy of the open market. To deny the goodwill and public spirit of all commercial managements would be unjust, but the record of omissions speaks for itself. It is as if key masterpieces in the National Gallery were withdrawn from circulation for years at a time, with this grim difference, that actors age quicker than paintings and cannot be restored. The most they can expect is preservation on film. Hence the importance of a system which keeps their best work in regular circulation.

Such a system had long been perfected abroad, on the foundations of subsidy, repertory and concentration of force. The fruits of it were demonstrated in London by the Comédie Française, the Moscow Art Theatre and the Berliner Ensemble. They confirmed the excellence of our Shakespearian star actors and no visiting actor improved on them. The visitors' superiority lay in teamwork and a pleasantly arrogant self-confidence reaching to the smallest parts. Everybody seemed to know exactly what they were about. The lesson was not lost on English actors. In 1957 Gielgud said that he envied the foreign companies their possession of a particular theatre building and ability to build up a stable repertory. That an actor of his eminence and achievement could take this attitude is of great significance. At the time he was playing in one of Noel Coward's less inspired comedies and he was soon to tour Shakespeare alone, in recitals. In neither role was he in the true relationship of a star Shakespearian actor to other actors and the public, scaling the heights of his art in a way to be remembered by the company on stage with him and the people in front. The likely conclusion is that adverse conditions had forced him out of circulation.

Other alternatives to improvised West End Shakespeare were offered by the expansion of air travel and a reservoir of audiences in, for example, Canada and the United States. This led to valuable pioneering, but increased the dispersal of talent. Another centrifugal influence was the attraction of television, aggravated by yet one more, the new pattern of filming on location abroad. The situation was summed up by an article in *The Times*,[1] headed *How we Waste our Best Actors*. 'There is plenty of labour being done, but exactly how far creative energy can be spread across different media and hemispheres without loss of quality is not yet known.' Three years later another article in the same paper,[2] gave an answer. 'The past year,' it began, 'has been unsatisfactory in a branch of drama which the English might be expected to excel in—that is, the performing of Shakespeare.' And the heading was *What is the Remedy for Bad Shakespearian Acting?* By that time the consequences of dispersal were becoming obvious. It had created a gap in the tradition of Shakespearian acting. Why had this not been filled by the Old Vic, back in Waterloo Road, and the Memorial Theatre at Stratford-on-Avon? Because neither could hold a company together long enough to consolidate. Casting had become a nightmare of detection, of tracking down actors in a network of airports, film and television studios, of co-ordinating engagements in several different media.

[1] *The Times,* 27 February 1959.
[2] *The Times,* 16 January 1962.

The city of Bradford, where Irving had died in 1905, saw no professional Shakespeare for more than eight years.

The gap was filled by directors, mostly wandering freelances like the actors and subject to the same distractions. With the example of Shakespearian stars absent, as it usually was, the younger directors and actors had to grope towards the most exacting plays in the language as best they could. The environment they shared was dominated by moving pictures, American Method acting and the English New Wave drama of 1956 onwards. Many things in the Shakespearian repertoire will yield to an approach on these lines, but they are no guide to aristocratic behaviour or the delivery of lyrical and rhetorical verse. One would have thought a suitable style could have been arrived at from a study of the text. However, it turned out otherwise, and it is only fair to add that younger French actors of the same period were known to mangle Racine just as badly. Regrettably, though, this deficiency was rarely admitted and the results were passed off as a valid recreation of the plays in modern terms. In fact they were an evasive distortion, masking incompetence.

One of innumerable examples was the Old Vic's rendering of *King John* III. i., where Constance laments her son and curses his murderers. This scene, one of the high points of Shakespeare's art, fell flat, and so, literally, did Maxine Audley, on the stage floor in spasms of grief. There are two points to note. On the first night, at any rate, several of her lines were inaudible. This is excusable in Method acting of plays in which the context may matter more than the lines as written, but Constance's lines in this scene were obviously written with care, if not inspiration, and the verse was clearly intended to bear the main weight of the action. Secondly, Miss Audley is a talented Shakespearian actress with full command of Shakespearian verse, as she proved in *Titus Andronicus* (1957) at the Stoll Theatre (capacity 2,400) where she was more audible than Olivier himself. For her Constance fiasco the blame must lie on the director, Peter Potter, whether the approach was her idea or his. It is evident at a glance that the episode will not yield to Method acting, unlike the Othello passage, already quoted. Another mystery was Miss Audley's disappointing Lady Macbeth. Or rather it would be a mystery, but for the connection I have indicated between acted Shakespeare and conditions working against it. Here was a beautiful actress with all the relevant experience, including Third Programme radio leads, fatal women in popular thrillers and Emilia to Orson Welles's Othello. Correctly applied, it must have added up to a splendid Lady Macbeth.

The waste of talent exemplified by Miss Audley's Old Vic appearances was echoed for an older generation by Wolfit's banishment to recitals, for a younger, by O'Toole's defection to films after a single season at Stratford-on-Avon. How far this waste was the fault of the actors concerned is not the point. The logic of the situation had become inescapable. A decade of Shakespearian acting talent ranging in age and style from Gielgud's Lear to O'Toole's Hamlet had failed to produce any revival comparable with the all-round standards of Glyndebourne and the Royal Ballet. Mozart had been better mounted than Shakespeare; Verdi's Othello had been better mounted than Shakespeare's; and on the international touring circuit, Chekhov and Brecht. The exceptional crop of stars, old and new, tended to mask the truth by improvised successes. But actors and directors new to Shakespeare inherited chaos. The truth was that the institutions formerly entrusted with the nurture of Shakespearian acting no longer sufficed. They had to be replaced.

Models for the new institutions were to hand. Essentially they conformed to Granville-Barker's blueprint for an exemplary theatre. The New and Haymarket seasons, the foreign visitors, the example of the ballet, had struck roots in England. Just in time, when shoddy presentation was in danger of classing Shakespeare as a bore, an archaic survival to be smuggled under a disguise of gimmicks, the means of presentation began to come under the control of those best fitted to understand them, the artists themselves. Olivier became director of the National Theatre, Brook and Saint-Denis directors of the Royal Shakespeare along with Peter Hall, who had extended the system of repertory and a permanent company from Stratford to the West End itself. John Neville, one of the best recent products of the defunct Old Vic, was appointed a co-director of the new civic theatre at Nottingham. In 1963 the way seemed clear for a concentration of forces in the best interests of Shakespearian acting. The battle had been won, at a price. By 1963, O'Toole and Finney, both on the brink of greatness, had not acted in Shakespeare for more than two years, Richard Burton for longer still. Some of the great actors and actresses were past their best. Spurious reputations, premature and dubious successes, had been won. Critical standards had fallen, because digestion adapts itself to a mediocre diet.

The bearing of all this on English studies, in which the actor's place as an interpreter is of some importance, need scarcely be insisted on. It would have been pleasanter to drape this study round a collection of jewelled performances, but that would have been to accept haphazard, hit-or-miss, attempts at what should be systematic. The roles of Hamlet and Macbeth should not be hawked around a competitive economy until the right man condescends to fit them in between a musical comedy and a film. They are a privilege, to be accepted in secure surroundings and enjoyed with humility. The proper conditions and atmosphere are now in sight. The artistic problems remain, and the worst of them spring from the absence of any recognized school of Shakespearian acting during the period, any blending of innovation and continuity.

Much could be learnt from an organization which grew up outside the focal points of contention, the National Youth Theatre. It was improvised by Michael Croft, a master at Alleyn's School, but on the sound principles of meaningful grouping, well drilled crowds and virile, eloquent speech. The company matured together, some of them through university and drama school, without dispersing until 1962 when the eldest were absorbed by professional drama and other careers. By that time the founder members had become the only Shakespearian ensemble in England and it would have been in the national interest to hold them together at any price. They had been well received in the West End and in Paris. Gielgud, Guinness, Redgrave, Bryam Shaw, Hall and Neville were on their council, with Richardson as president. But in the lean, declining years of the Old Vic, Croft was never invited to direct there, nor at Stratford-on-Avon. It was as if those in charge of Shakespeare's theatrical headquarters had little confidence in a director committed first and foremost to Shakespeare's text.